Libel on Trial:
The Westmoreland and Sharon Cases

A BNA Special Report

Poynter Institute for Media Studies
Library

JAN 1 4 '87

The Bureau of National Affairs, Inc. 1231 25th Street, N.W., Washington, D.C. 200037

LIBEL ON TRIAL

A BNA Special Report on the Westmoreland and Sharon Cases

ISBN:0-87179-495-0

Extra copies of this report are available for $35 from BNA's Research and Special Projects Division, 1231 25th St., N.W., Washington, D.C. 20037, telephone (toll-free) 1-800-452-7773. In the Washington area, call 452-4323. Discounts are available for orders of six or more copies.

Copyright ©1985
The Bureau of National Affairs, Inc.

LIBEL ON TRIAL

In the fall of 1984, two trials occupied the attention not only of the media bar but of the entire nation: the trial of Gen. William Westmoreland's libel action against CBS (*Westmoreland v. CBS*, No. 82 Civ. 7913) and the trial of Israeli Gen. Ariel Sharon's libel suit against Time (*Sharon v. Time*, No. 83 Civ. 4660). *Newsweek* magazine, in a cover story, called the *Westmoreland* case "the libel trial of the century," and similar labels were applied to *Sharon*. Both cases generated numerous published decisions during the pre-trial and trial stages (4 in *Sharon*, 8 in *Westmoreland*), but both cases ended abruptly, with the *Sharon* case culminating in a jury verdict that will not be appealed, and with Westmoreland agreeing to drop his action prior to submission of the case to the jury. Yet the trials of these two cases can provide lawyers and judges with fresh insights into the handling of complex libel litigation. This special report examines the two trials, with emphasis on the procedures used which could affect similar trials in the future.

Background

Westmoreland

On January 23, 1982, CBS broadcast a documentary entitled "The Uncounted Enemy: A Vietnam Deception." The documentary concerned U.S. estimates of enemy troop strength during the Vietnam War. Gen. William Westmoreland, who served as commander of the U.S. Military Assistance Command, Vietnam, contended that the central theme of the broadcast defamed him by asserting that he had led a conspiracy to suppress and distort intelligence as to the size of the enemy's forces. On September 13, 1982, Westmoreland, represented by Dan Burt, of the Capital Legal Foundation in Washington, and by David M. Dorsen, of Sachs, Greenebaum & Tayler, Washington, sued CBS and certain individuals involved in the broadcast, including correspondent Mike Wallace and George Crile, the show's producer. CBS was represented by David Boies, of New York's Cravath, Swaine & Moore. Crile retained Victor Kovner, of Lankenau Kovner & Bickford, New York. Westmoreland's suit was filed initially in the U.S. District Court for the District of South Carolina, but in November 1982 that court granted CBS's motion for a change of venue to the U.S. District Court for the Southern District of New York (8 Med.L.Rptr. 2493). The case was assigned to Judge Pierre Leval, who had been appointed to the federal bench in 1978 by President Carter.

Other pre-trial decisions in the *Westmoreland* case include the following:

▶*Internal reports*. CBS resisted the disclosure during discovery of an internal report that was prepared in July 1982 by Burton Benjamin, a CBS senior executive producer. The report was submitted to CBS News President Van Gordon Sauter, who in a public memorandum that was released July 15, 1982, and that was cited by Westmoreland in his complaint as an additional defamatory statement, declared that the network "stands by this broadcast." Judge Pierre Leval granted Westmoreland's motion to compel production of the Benjamin report (9 Med.L.Rptr. 1521), noting that CBS had not treated the report as a confidential internal memorandum but had in fact relied on the report's conclusions for "public justification" of the broadcast. Westmoreland then sought disclosure of drafts of the Benjamin report, as well as of Benjamin's interview notes and other material received by him during the course of his investigation. Again, the motions to compel were granted (9 Med.L.Rptr. 2316, 10 Med.L.Rptr. 1215), although Leval noted that CBS need not identify two military officers who were interviewed during the investigation, who were promised confidentiality, and whose names had already been furnished to Westmoreland as sources for the documentary. He also specified that Benjamin's notes were to be held by plaintiff's counsel in confidence and were to be used solely in preparation for trial.

▶ *Camera coverage.* On the eve of trial, the Cable News Network asked Leval for permission to broadcast the proceedings. All parties to the litigation agreed that cameras should be permitted, and Leval himself noted that, in view of the public issues raised by the case, the filming of the trial might conceivably be more important than the trial itself. He ruled, however, that the federal rules prohibiting broadcast coverage permitted him no discretion as to coverage but required him to deny the application (10 Med.L.Rptr. 2386). That decision was affirmed by the U.S. Court of Appeals for the Second Circuit (11 Med.L.Rptr. 1013).

▶ *Summary judgment.* On September 24, 1984, Leval denied CBS's motion for summary judgment (10 Med.L.Rptr. 2417), holding that the network had failed to demonstrate the absence of a genuine issue of material fact. Leval noted instances cited by Westmoreland in support of his contention that CBS acted with "willful falsity in the editing and presentation of evidence." These instances, he said, "sufficiently raise triable questions of knowing or reckless falsity to foreclose summary judgment on the issue of constitutional malice." Leval also refused to rule, in the context of a summary judgment motion, on CBS's assertion that it should be absolutely immune from libel actions brought by high public officials, based upon commentary concerning their discharge of their official duties. CBS argued that requiring a media organization to defend such a lawsuit is functionally equivalent to the prosecution of a seditious libel claim. It would be "inappropriate" to rule on such "novel contentions" in advance of trial, Leval said, noting that no precedent supported CBS's contention. This assertion could be renewed by CBS at the conclusion of the trial, Leval said, an event which was, of course, foreclosed by the case's settlement.

▶ *"Actual Malice."* In his opinion denying summary judgment, Leval also raised his concern over the possible prejudice that might be caused by use of the term "actual malice." That term "carries a significant potential for prejudice," Leval said, suggesting that a "more neutral" word be chosen, a suggestion which later would result in an order directing that "state of mind" be used rather than "actual malice."

On October 9, 1984, trial began. After more than four months of trial, the action was discontinued on February 18, 1985, with the parties agreeing in a joint statement that "their respective positions have been effectively placed before the public for its consideration and that continuing the legal process at this stage would serve no further purpose." In the joint statement, CBS said it "respects General Westmoreland's long and faithful service to his country and never intended to assert, and does not believe, that General Westmoreland was unpatriotic or disloyal in performing his duties as he saw them." Westmoreland said he "respects the long and distinguished journalistic tradition of CBS and the rights of journalists to examine the complex issues of Vietnam and to present perspectives contrary to his own."

Sharon

On February 21, 1983, *Time* published an article entitled "The Verdict is Guilty." The article reported on the findings and recommendations made by Israel's Kahan Commission, which was appointed to investigate the massacre of Palestinian refugees in the Sabra and Shatilla refugee camps in West Beirut, Lebanon. The article said that the commission reserved its "strongest condemnation" for former defense minister Ariel Sharon. In the only paragraph alleged by Sharon to be libelous, the magazine stated:

"One section of the report, known as Appendix B, was not published at all, mainly for security reasons. That section contains the names of several intelligence agents referred to elsewhere in the report. TIME has learned that it also contains further details about Sharon's visit to the Gemayel family on the day after Bashir Gemayel's assassination. Sharon reportedly told the Gemayels that the Israeli army would be moving into West Beirut and that he expected the Christian forces to go into the Palestinian refugee camps. Sharon also reportedly discussed with the Gemayels the need for the Phalangists to take revenge for the assassination of Bashir, but the details of the conversation are not known."

Sharon, represented by Milton S. Gould, of the New York City firm of Shea & Gould, filed suit. Time was represented by Thomas D. Barr, of Cravath, Swaine & Moore. The *Sharon* case was assigned to Judge Abraham Sofaer, who had been appointed to the bench in 1979 by President Carter. Pre-trial decisions growing out of this litigation included:

▶*Motion to dismiss.* In December 1983, Sofaer denied Time's motion to dismiss (10 Med.L.Rptr. 1146). The article, Sofaer said, could, when read in context, lead a reasonable reader to believe that the secret "Appendix B" contained additional material adverse to Sharon, it could suggest that Sharon condoned the massacre, and it could imply that Sharon, who had claimed not to have considered the possibility of such violence, had lied. Sofaer also rejected Time's assertion that Sharon was "libel proof." It was true, he noted, that Sharon's reputation as a political and military leader had been "severely affected" by the unchallenged facts as reported in the article. "Nevertheless," Sofaer ruled, "his reputation cannot be said as a matter of law to have been so damaged by the reported events that he could recover only nominal damages for the article's potentially libelous statements."

▶*Discovery.* On September 5, 1984, Sofaer defined the extent to which Time could discover evidence concerning alleged "prior similar acts" by Sharon (11 Med.L.Rptr. 1044). Time sought discovery in certain broad categories, including Sharon's record of, and reputation for, "vicious brutality toward Arab civilians," his record regarding "excessive personal ambition and a willingness to use any means to advance his political career," and Sharon's "determination to make war in Lebanon and his role in expanding the war beyond the scope authorized" by the Israeli prime minister and cabinet. Time must properly be permitted to discover, Sofaer said, unprivileged information as to what the Kahan report stated concerning the details of Sharon's meeting with the Gemayels, as well as any information concerning Sharon's version of that meeting. Time was told that it could seek any nonprivileged information possessed by Sharon which concerned his alleged plan to use the Phalange in Sabra and Shatilla, although Sofaer noted that Sharon's obligation to provide information "may perhaps be limited by Israeli security laws," and in fact Sharon would later refuse to testify as to certain matters. Information as to alleged "other acts" by Sharon would not directly prove either that Sharon in fact had the conversation with the Gemayels which Time reported, Sofaer said, or that the Kahan report described the details of such a conversation. Only those aspects of the "other acts" categories "which may shed relevant light on Time's lack of actual malice, or on the question of damages, are properly discoverable," he said.

▶*Bifurcation.* As part of the same September 5, 1984, opinion, Sofaer raised the possibility of a bifurcated trial. "The significant differences in the evidence that will be admissible on truth or falsity, on the one hand, and on malice or damages, on the other, and the complications and likely inability of the jury to avoid giving improper consideration to some potentially prejudicial evidence in this case at this point makes a bifurcated trial seem more efficient and just than a single-stage trial," he said in asking the parties to brief the bifurcation question. In an order handed down October 9, Sofaer concluded that bifurcation, in the sense of having two separate trials and two separate juries, "would be inappropriate." Bifurcation would not enhance judicial economy, convenience, or fairness, he said. "The interest in avoiding prejudice might well have been served by bifurcation if a line could effectively have been drawn between evidence relating to the truth of the alleged libel, and evidence relating to the plaintiff's reputation," Sofaer said. He noted that bifurcation could "significantly prejudice" Time, since "if the first stage of trial was limited to the issue of truth...then the jury might never be presented with much of the evidence concerning reputation. This segregation would serve the needs of plaintiffs who are primarily concerned with establishing falsity, and who therefore might discontinue their suits after a trial on truth. But trial procedures in libel cases, particularly those involving public figures and public issues, should not be designed to encourage suits aimed at establishing only falsity. The constitutional rules governing liability in libel cases were designed both to protect defendants from adverse judgments and to protect them from the costs and chilling effects of trials. Plaintiffs should not be encouraged by the possible use of bifurcation to sue with the hope of obtaining separate, preliminary verdicts on truth or falsity."

However, after the trial began, Sofaer directed that any material relevant to damages suffered by Sharon would be admissible only after the jury returned with its verdict on the fact of injury—whether the Time paragraph was false and defamatory and whether Time had published it with actual malice. This division, according to Time attorney Stuart Gold, of Cravath, Swaine & Moore, was a "horrible" idea that would have been challenged by the magazine had an appeal been taken. This division precluded Time from introducing evidence relating to Sharon's character, and "gave Sharon the upper hand in the public relations battle."

▶*Act of state.* The unusual aspect of a public official of a foreign government suing in an American court led not only to disputes concerning the availability of evidence from Israel, but also to the question of whether the entire lawsuit was barred by the act of state doctrine. On November 12, Sofaer denied Time's request to dismiss the lawsuit based on that doctrine (11 Med.L.Rptr. 1153). Neither Sharon's alleged actions, nor the findings of the Kahan commission, nor Israel's alleged participation in the lawsuit "constitutes an act of state within the meaning of the doctrine," the court said.

▶*Sharon Testimony.* As part of that same ruling, Sofaer held that Sharon's refusal to answer certain deposition questions, particularly on what is contained in the report's Appendix B, based on his assertion that to do so would be to violate Israeli security requirements, did not preclude him from testifying at trial about those subjects, since that privilege is "soundly based in foreign law," and since the importance of the withheld testimony was largely mitigated by the availability of other evidence.

▶*Summary Judgment.* In his November 12 decision, Sofaer also denied Time's motion for summary judgment. "The record contains sufficient admissible evidence of actual malice to preclude summary judgment," he ruled. In part, Sofaer took into account the refusal of Time's Israel correspondent, David Halevy, to reveal his confidential sources of information concerning what happened at the meeting between Sharon and the Gemayel family at Bikfaya. Although Sofaer held that Halevy's refusal to disclose his sources could not, under the New York shield law, preclude him from testifying at trial that he obtained the information from persons he considered to be trustworthy, he added that the shield law "is a shield, and no more." Halevy's "reliance on the shield law has left the record in a state that precludes summary judgment in Time's favor," Sofaer said.

▶*Due Process.* As part of its summary judgment motion, Time argued that its inability to obtain necessary information from Israel and from Sharon constituted a denial of due process. Time's assertions, Sofaer said, "are based on Time's exaggerated view of the relevant issues, and its unproven claim that Israel is somehow working with General Sharon to prevent Time from gaining access to documents and witnesses. In fact, Time has available to it a huge amount of evidence to set even its broadest claim, and the State of Israel has thus far reacted to the requests placed before it in a manner consistent with a good faith desire to cooperate while at the same time preventing the unwarranted disclosure—intentional or inadvertent—of materials its laws normally mandate be kept confidential." Time continued during the trial to assert its due process claims, although Sofaer reserved judgment on that claim.

An attempt to obtain documents from the Kahan commission led to a separate issue in the trial involving courtroom closure. After both sides had rested their cases, Sofaer continued efforts to obtain the documents from Israel, and an agreement was reached where one Israeli attorney representing each side was permitted to review certain documents in the presence of Israeli Supreme Court President Justice Yitzhak Kahan, who had served as chairman of the investigating commission. Kahan also answered questions put forth by Sofaer and the litigants, saying that the commission had not found any evidence that Sharon had discussed revenge with the Gemayel family. Time objected that its attorneys were not given access to certain testimony presented at the commission hearings.

Under the agreement, Kahan's answers, together with "reservations" written after the meeting with Kahan by Time's Israeli attorney, Haim Zadok, could be released only to the court. Israel later disclosed Kahan's answers on its own, but the pact still covered what became known as the "Zadok" reservations. Sofaer sought permission to disclose that material, but he said in court January 8 that the process to obtain that permission would be lengthy, requiring meetings of two Knesset committees and permission of four cabinet members.

In order to admit the document into evidence and present it to the jury, Sofaer said he had to interpret the agreement broadly. A resolution of the Israeli cabinet called for release of the documents only to "the court." Sofaer said that he would interpret "the court" to include the jury. However, he said, until the Israeli government permitted public release, the document would be sealed, and the press and public would be excluded from the courtroom when the material was presented to the jury.

Several news organizations appealed that closure ruling to the U.S. Court of Appeals for the Second Circuit. The Israeli government then decided, however, to permit release of the material, and, as a result, Sofaer lifted his order. The Second Circuit subsequently ruled that the issue was moot.

Time continues to feel that it was denied due process, according to Harry M. Johnston, III, general counsel of Time's Magazine Group. He predicted that the issue of gaining access to government information in order to defend a libel action may become critical even in cases that do not involve a foreign government, in view of the increasing use of secrecy agreements involving U.S. government officials. "It's hard to imagine a federal official who hasn't signed some sort of secrecy agreement," Johnston said. If public officials are encouraged, through the use of special verdicts or a change in libel laws, to bring libel suits to obtain simply a declaration of truth or falsity, media organizations may be hard pressed to obtain the necessary evidence on truth, Johnston said. One possible solution may be that devised by the U.S. District Court for the District of Columbia in *Phillips v. Freed* (11 Med.L.Rptr. 1311). David Atlee Phillips, a former Central Intelligence Agency employee, refused, during pre-trial discovery in his libel action against the authors and publishers of a book concerning the assassination of Orlando Letelier, to answer more than 160 questions, asserting that his answers would violate the terms of his CIA secrecy agreement. The Justice Department also appeared at the deposition and objected, on national security grounds, to any order compelling disclosure. The district court refused the defendants' motion to dismiss the suit, but it did order that, "in view of defendant's failure, whether through unwillingness or inability," to disclose information, certain facts should be assumed to have been established.

Trial began on October 29, 1984, and lasted through January. The jury deliberated for 11 days. In separate announcements, it concluded that the article was false, and that it was defamatory. On January 24, it returned its final verdict with the finding that the statement had not been shown to have been published with actual malice. In a separate statement accompanying the verdict, however, the jury said that "we find that certain Time employees, particularly David Halevy, acted negligently and carelessly in reporting and verifying the information which ultimately found its way into the published paragraph of interest in this case."

TRIAL INNOVATIONS

Both trials featured a number of innovative features, features that will doubtless be used again, not only in libel trials but in litigation practice generally. The procedures used which were favorably received include the following:

Voir Dire

In both cases, the juries were selected in under a day—an amazingly speedy process which attorneys attributed to the effective use of screening devices, such as the jury questionnaire which was used in *Sharon* and which is reprinted as Appendix 6. Leval used an unofficial "checklist" to screen jurors, and he also permitted attorneys to do a limited degree of questioning which, although not completely unheard of, is somewhat unusual in the Southern District, where the judge usually handles the voir dire alone.

Under the procedure adopted by Leval, counsel for each side were permitted, during each challenge round, to question jurors for a total of one minute multiplied by the number of new jurors in the round. Thus, during the opening round in which 18 new jurors were offered, each side was permitted 18 minutes. If, during a subsequent round, 4 new jurors were offered, then each side would be given four additional minutes, although Leval specified that the questions could be addressed to any juror and need not be restricted to newly impanelled jurors. This questioning, Leval said, would be permitted "solely because of the recognition that counsel will be better able to uncover latent hostilities and prejudices than the judge's formal neutral questions." He added, however, that questioning by counsel is "susceptible to abuses which will not be permitted. It is not to be used to preview the evidence, to curry favor or sympathy with jurors, to impart favorable information or to instill hostility towards the adversary, etc.," and he warned that "abuses may lead to forfeiture of the right to question further or other appropriate redress."

David Dorsen, one of Westmoreland's lawyers, said that the lawyer questioning was not "terribly useful," possibly because most of the attorneys were experienced in trial work at the federal level, where such questioning is not the rule, rather than in state trials.

In the *Westmoreland* case, Westmoreland employed a jury consultant, but CBS did not. CBS "piggybacked" on much of the work done by the plaintiff, according to George Vradenburg, III, CBS associate general counsel, in that the CBS attorneys acted on the answers and reactions given by jurors to questions asked by the plaintiff. "We found that persons who would respect Westmoreland would also respect Mike Wallace," Vradenburg said, since Wallace is perceived "as someone who would protect the little guy."

Victor Kovner, who represented defendant George Crile in *Westmoreland*, noted that the Southern District—in which both cases were tried—is not a completely urban district, even though the courthouse is located in Manhattan. Of the 12 jurors selected in *Westmoreland*, Kovner noted that 7 were from New York City, and five were from upstate counties, such as Westchester, Putnam, and Rockland.

Interim Summations

In the *Westmoreland* case, Leval directed that the two sides would each have a total of two hours over the course of the trial to make interim statements to the jury (for full text of Leval's order on interim summations, see Appendix 2). The attorneys were given discretion as to when these interim statements would be given, although they were cautioned that the use of such summations "may not unreasonably interfere with the opposing party's presentation or with the court's schedule."

Interim summations, according to attorneys involved in the case, represented a valuable way to underline points to the jury at the time when an issue was immediately before it. Victor Kovner noted that the *Westmoreland* trial began in October, but the defendant's case didn't get underway until January. "This is a long time for the jury to hear just the plaintiff's case," he noted, but the interim summations represented one way for the defendants to get their points across. Interim summations "give you a few minutes with the jurors, while they're thinking about a particular point, rather than having to wait for several months," according to Stuart Gold, who said that he was not "initially enthusiastic" about the idea of interim summations but has "now embraced" the concept.

David Dorsen, who handled two interim summations during the trial, said that interim summations are "a potentially very useful tool," in that they allow a greater degree of communcation between counsel and jury. The device "needs more people thinking" about how best it should be employed, he said.

"X-Chart"

If use of interim summations was one useful tool for lawyers to communicate with the jury, another helpful device used by Leval in explaining the evidence was an "X Chart." The chart was divided into four quadrants: state of mind, truth/falsity, state of mind and truth, and other issues (such as the credibility of witnesses). As testimony was given, Leval told the jurors in which quadrant of the chart the evidence was admissible. The X-Chart was a "vivid and informative way" of letting the jury know what the evidence was, Dorsen said.

Time Limits

Leval, in addition to setting two hours as the maximum time available for interim summations, specified that each side would have a total of 150 hours for the presentation of evidence throughout the trial, including direct examination, cross examination, presentation of exhibits, argument of exhibits, etc. This 150-hour limit was established by Leval, after discussion and negotiations with counsel, and was based upon estimates submitted by the parties prior to trial as to the time that would be needed to try the case. Attorneys agree that the restriction was a vital factor in keeping the trial within a manageable time frame. Without these time limits, the case "could have gone on till July," Kovner said. Coping with a time restriction requires effective pre-planning by counsel. "It forces attorneys to think about what they're doing," according to Dorsen, who called the time restriction the "single most important innovation" in the *Westmoreland* trial.

During the trial, Leval would call the attorneys in to check on the amount of time each side had remaining. Toward the end of the trial, Westmoreland attorney Dan Burt used approximately 25 hours in his questioning of George Crile, the CBS producer who was called by Burt as a hostile witness. Running short of time, Burt asked that each side be given five additional hours. In ruling on the requested time extension, Leval noted that both sides had agreed that the issue of whether additional time be granted should be resolved mutually, "so that after the verdict no claim could be made by either side (or its partisans) that it has been prejudiced by the court's awarding or denying additional time." The parties agreed that if the plaintiff reached the 150-hour limit, he would be allowed, for each subsequent witness, time for cross-examination equal to the time used by the defendant on direct examination. Such negotiations among counsel are necessary in administering a time limitation, Leval noted after the trial. He said that in the future he would make clear in advance that the time restrictions would be administered flexibly.

Note-taking by Jurors

Another device used by Leval which was somewhat unusual was encouraging the jurors to take notes during the trial, in order to help them keep clear which evidence was relevant for state of mind, for truth, etc. In a long trial, Dorsen said, this may be of some advantage to the plaintiff, because the notes enable jurors to go back, during the presentation of the defendant's testimony, and refresh their recollection of the plaintiff's evidence on that point. One possible drawback to note-taking is the risk that the more aggressive jurors will be the most assiduous note-takers, and that too much importance might ultimately be attached to those notes.

Leval also did not tell the jury not to watch television or read the newspapers during the course of the trial, in view of the difficulty of isolating jurors from news reports concerning such a highly-publicized trial. He rather instructed the jurors not to be influenced by what they saw or read, emphasizing the fact that they knew more of what was going on during the trial than what was reported in the news accounts.

"State of Mind"

In his order denying CBS's motion for summary judgment, Leval indicated in a footnote his belief that use of the term "actual malice" during the trial could cause confusion and prejudice. The possibility of confusion, Leval said, "is not so pernicious in written judicial opinions, since these are read primarily by lawyers and make clear that the words are used only as a code symbolizing the element. The problem is far more serious, however, in the context of a jury trial where the use of the term malice, or worse—actual malice—carries a significant potential for prejudice...If jurors are repeatedly told througout the trial that evidence is being received on the issue of 'malice,' they are likely to find an unwarranted liability notwithstanding the few instances when the court instructs at length." In this case, Leval said, "actual malice" carries the risk of significant prejudice to the defendants, in view of the undisputed fact that defendant Samuel Adams—the prime CBS source for the broadast—had "persistently harbored and advanced his accusations" against Westmoreland since 1967, including filing a complaint with the Army's Inspector General charging Westmoreland with court martial offenses.

A "more neutral" word should be used, Leval said, suggesting the following possibilities: "constitutional limitation," "state of mind," "deliberate or reckless falsity," "abuse of privilege," and "impermissible basis." In an order filed October 29, Leval chose the term "state of mind" as the "most appropriate label to use in the presence of the jury to identify the element described in *New York Times v. Sullivan*, 376 U.S. 272 [1 Med.L.Rptr. 1527] (1964) and other leading cases as 'actual malice.' I believe this term is more precise and less likely to inflict prejudice than the others considered."

Use of the "state of mind" term was "probably helpful," Dorsen said. "There's no reason to use a term that is potentially confusing" when an alternative is available, he said. Gold, who was involved to some extent in both the trials, indicated that he "didn't see much difference" attributable to using "state of mind" rather than "actual malice." He noted, however, that both trials featured sophisticated juries and judges who understood the law well. "With the right jury, and a judge who takes time, juries can understand what actual malice means," Gold said.

Jury Instructions

The jury instructions proposed for use in *Westmoreland* were, of course, never given. In *Sharon*, the instructions went through at least five drafts for comments by counsel, and were considered during three oral arguments. The instructions as given (published in Appendix 4) were praised by many as an effective means of guiding the jury through the maze of determining falsity, defamatory content, and actual malice, although counsel for Time were not completely swayed. "I was not at all happy" with the instructions, Stuart Gold said, although he added that the final instructions were "much better than what we started out with."

Among the passages most strongly objected to by Time, according to Gold, which was deleted from the final set of instrcutions, was a paragraph which would have permitted the jury to find for Sharon even if he was unable to prove that any single individual responsible for the paragraph acted with actual malice. This concept of "corporate malice," Time said, in a memorandum concerning the proposed instructions, "posits an abstraction without form or substance, and simply short cuts the actual malice requirement." Time was less successful in revamping what it felt was the "road map to actual malice" set forth in the instructions. The final instructions somewhat "watered down" this "road map," Gold said. The instructions, he said, "were carefully thought out, and spelled out Sofaer's view of the law for the jury," but, he said, "I wouldn't consider them a model for future use."

The Westmoreland instructions as printed in Appendix 2 are the second draft given to counsel for comments.

Kovner said the instructions' language on defamatory content was "good," but, he said, it was "troublesome" that Leval's instructions specified that the jury could consider whether the allegedly defamatory accusations were made "*by inference* as well as by explicit statement."

Tripartite Verdicts

In *Sharon*, the jury was instructed to return a special verdict divided into three segments: defamatory meaning, falsity, and actual malice. More unusually, the verdicts were each announced separately. In part, this "multiple reporting" of the special verdict was caused by Sofaer's uncertainty over whether Sharon must prove falsity by clear and convincing evidence, or simply by a preponderance of the evidence. Under the instructions given, the jury was asked whether Sharon had proved falsity by "clear and convincing" evidence, to which the jurors answered "yes." Had the jury returned a "no" answer to that question, Sofaer was apparently prepared to re-instruct the jury to determine whether falsity had been shown by a preponderance of the evidence.

Had the jury returned each of the verdicts quickly, over a matter of a few hours, the effect might not have been so striking. Instead, however, the verdicts came down on separate days, and each was the object of news attention, thus perhaps giving greater effect to Sharon's "winning" the first two segments than would have been the case had the verdicts been returned simultaneously or in rapid succession.

In *Westmoreland*, the plaintiff sought a general verdict rather than a special verdict, without any objection from CBS. Leval, however, insisted on the use of a special verdict, asserting that to do otherwise would "pervert the processes of the system." He yielded, however, on the question of separately announcing the verdicts; in the proposed jury instructions, he noted that "the court would have preferred separate announcements as done in *Sharon v. Time, Inc.*, but yields to the joint request of the parties."

Westmoreland sought a general, rather than a special, verdict, for a number of reasons, most notably perhaps the reluctance to risk losing on the issue of truth, which would have been much more devastating to him than simply losing a general verdict. In addition, Dorsen said, "I felt we were more likely to win everything if the jury wasn't focused on separate issues."

Why did CBS also seek a general verdict? "The common wisdom," according to Vradenburg, "is that a jury will tend to compromise when the case is close and there is a sympathetic plaintiff. On a special verdict, this would mean that a jury would give the truth issue to the plaintiff and the actual malice issue to the defendant. We did not want to give the jury an opportunity to compromise" on the truth issue. For media organizations, Vradenburg said, "to lose on truth is damaging, even if you ultimately win on actual malice."

Reaction to the three-step approach used in *Sharon* has been generally positive. That procedure is "uncommon, but will become more common," according to Bruce Sanford, of Baker and Hostetler, Washington, D.C., who added that the approach is "logical and sensible and correct analytically." Robert D. Sack, of Patterson, Belknap, Webb & Tyler, New York City, agreed that "it makes a lot of sense" to structure the verdict in three separate parts, although he added that he was unsure as to the impact that procedure might have on libel litigation. "It's a good development for libel defendants since, by separating out the charges, it makes it easier for juries to focus on actual malice," he said. "Yet it also makes it easier for a plaintiff to vindicate his or her reputation without overcoming the actual malice standard, so that could end up encouraging lawsuits." Floyd Abrams, of Cahill, Gordon & Reindel, New York City, in a speech to the American Newspaper Publishers Association's Government Affairs Committee, urged media attorneys to "push, on a case-by-case basis, for expanded uses of special questions to jurors and—as Judge Sofaer did—separate responses by jurors as they reach their verdicts on each question."

The verdict approach used in *Sharon* has spurred additional thinking on how libel law should accommodate public official lawsuits. Rep. Charles Schumer (D-NY), a member of the House Judiciary Committee's Civil and Constitutional Rights Subcommittee, has begun to explore the possibility of hearings and legislation to address these issues. One legislative proposal currently being considered by Schumer would eliminate punitive damages in all libel cases, would provide for the award of attorneys' fees to the prevailing party in a libel case, and would establish a new cause of action that would essentially provide a judicial declaration on the truth and defamatory impact of the allegedly libelous statement. The plaintiff in such an action would be precluded from obtaining damages, but would also not have to demonstrate that the statement was published with actual malice.

Professor Marc Franklin of the Stanford University Law School has suggested a similar approach: retain the actual malice standard for suits in which plaintiffs want to seek damages, but offer a "simpler, faster, and less expensive" route for plaintiffs who want simply to vindicate their reputation. Such vindication, some have suggested, could occur through a nonbinding arbitration procedure, which would focus on the truth or falsity of the statement at issue, rather than on the alleged fairness or unfairness of the publication.

APPENDIX 1

Westmoreland v. CBS

Order on Interim Summations and Time Limits

October 3, 1984

1. *Interim Summations.* Plaintiff and defendants as a group (hereinafter "defendants") will each have a total of two hours over the course of the trial to make interim statements to the jury. When such time will be utilized is at counsel's discretion, except that it may not unreasonably interfere with the opposing party's presentation or with the court's schedule. The parties shall keep a record of time expended.

2. Plaintiff and defendants will each have 150 hours for the presentation of evidence throughout the trial, including direct examination, cross examination, presentation of exhibits, argument of objections, et al. Time will run from the start through the conclusion of each day's proceedings with time out for lunch. The parties shall keep records of time expended.

3. Plaintiff and defendants will advise one another on Thursday, October 4, 1984 by 8 p.m. of excerpts from exhibits that they intend to use in opening statements. Objections to such excerpts will be exchanged by October 7, 1984 by 10 a.m. Counsel are encouraged to reach accommodation.

4. On October 5, 1984 plaintiff will designate its witnesses with allocation of approximate time for direct examination, and designation in gross of the utilization of additional time. Defendants will make a similar designation on October 10, 1984.

5. The parties will deliver a list of designated exhibits to the court by October 8, 1984 at 8 p.m. Objections to admissibility and other limitations will be specified by October 10, 1984 at 8 p.m. The final list should be in numerical order, presented as follows:
   Exhibit Number
   Brief Description
   Specification of Objections
   Leave Blank for Court Notations

6. It is noted for the record that counsel were informed on Tuesday, September 18, 1984 that the father of my new law clerk Kathleen Pickering served as Special Assistant to Ambassador Ellsworth Bunker in Saigon from June 1968 to June 1970 when Ms. Pickering was nine years old. Ms. Pickering stated that her father did not discuss the substance of his work in Vietnam with her, and that she did not live in Saigon during this period but did make brief visits to her father there. Counsel for the parties stated that they did not object to Ms. Pickering serving as my law clerk on the case.

APPENDIX 2

Westmoreland v. CBS

Proposed Jury Instructions

Members of the Jury:

If you can remember as far back as the start of this trial, you will recall that I spoke to you of the great power that you hold as jurors and of the great importance of your exercising that power with complete fairness.

You must decide the issues of fact solely on the basis of the evidence presented in the trial.

You may not allow yourselves to be influenced by opinions you had at the start of trial.

You must put aside opinions you may have had concerning the military; the Vietnam War; General Westmoreland; the CIA; the press; CBS; Mike Wallace and any others.

I told you at the start, if your decision were to be based on your opinions, we didn't need a trial. We could simply select the jury and ask them for the verdict. This is not the way it is done. The trial has been conducted in a most painstaking manner to place evidence before you. Your verdict is to be based on that evidence. You promised on the first day, during jury selection, that you would put any opinions and preferences aside and would decide on the evidence. Now you must fulfill those promises.

I. *The Elements*

In order to win your verdict, plaintiff must prove each of the following elements:

I. The defendants' broadcast published a defamatory statement or message.

II. The defamatory statement was "of and concerning" the plaintiff — which means it was about the plaintiff personally.

III. The defamatory statement about the plaintiff was false.

IV. The defendants published the false defamatory statement about plaintiff either knowing it to be false or with reckless disregard whether it was false.

V. Plaintiff's reputation was damaged by the publication of the false defamatory statement.

I remind you when I speak of publishing a statement. I mean nothing more than making it public. It is agreed by both sides that the defendants' documentary, and everything in it, was "published" when it was broadcast on January 23, 1982.

In a moment I will explain in detail each of these elements, except the last — damages — which I will leave till later. You will not consider the question of damages at this stage of your deliberations.

II. *Public Official — Special Rules*

Because General Westmoreland held public office and was a public figure, a libel action brought by him goes under different rules from a libel action brought by an ordinary citizen in private life.

The law recognizes conflicting interests, both of which are entitled protection. On the one side, the law recognizes the legitimate interest of any person to be protected against publication of false defamatory statements about him.

On the other hand, the law recognizes that it is important to all of us in a free democracy that there should be free, open discussion in the press of the actions of our public officials. If the press incurred liability whenever a derogatory report about a public official turned out to be wrong, regardless whether it was published in the good faith belief that it was true, the press might be afraid to risk critical commentary, and we the public would be less informed.

For public officials, the law strikes a compromise that protects a measure of the public official's interest in a remedy against false slander, but protects also the public's interest in being able to see open good-faith discussion of the performance of public officials in the press.

Under this compromise, the public official retains the right to bring a libel action for false defamatory statements of fact about him, but he must prove more than merely that the statement was false. He must prove also that a defendant acted with what we have referred to as the prohibited state of mind, that the defendant published the false defamatory statement knowing it to be false, or with reckless disregard of whether it was false.

III. Burdens of Proof

That compromise also imposes on the public-official-plaintiff a more demanding burden of proof than is customary in other civil cases.

The phrase "burden of proof" refers to the obligation to persuade the jury.

It is used in two senses: first to identify which party must persuade the jury; secondly, it sets the standard of how firmly convinced the jury must be before it may render a verdict in favor of the party who bears the burden of proof.

As to the first question, the burden of proof is on the plaintiff. That means — if the plaintiff has not convinced you of any issue, you must find for the defendants on that issue. And if plaintiff does not prove every element to you, you must award the verdict to the defendants.

The second question is: How firmly must you be convinced before you may find for the plaintiff on any issue? The answer is not the same for each of the elements. I just listed for you the five elements that plaintiff must prove in order to win your verdict. As to the first and the last, there is one standard; as to the third and fourth, falsity and the defendants' state of mind, there is another.

As to the question (i) whether the statements made by the broadcast had a defamatory meaning, (ii) whether those statements were about General Westmoreland, and (v) whether his reputation was harmed or damaged by those statements, plaintiff must prove those elements to you — "*by a fair preponderance of the evidence.*"

What do we mean by a "fair preponderance of the evidence"? A fact has been demonstrated by a fair preponderance of the evidence if, after considering all the relevant evidence, you find it more probable than not that the fact is true. You judge this by the quality and persuasiveness of the evidence.

If the evidence persuades you that a questioned fact was more likely true than not, then the party who has the burden of proving that fact has met his burden of proof as to the fact. If, however, the evidence is evenly balanced between the parties so that you cannot decide whether the fact is true or not, then the party who has the burden of proof has failed to meet his burden and you must find that fact against him.

As to the third and fourth elements — whether the broadcast's statement was false — and whether the defendants published with the prohibited state of mind, plaintiff must prove these elements to you by "clear and convincing evidence".

Clear and convincing evidence is a more exacting standard than proof by a *preponderance of the evidence*. Clear and convincing proof leaves no substantial doubt in your mind. It is proof that establishes in your mind not only that the existence of a fact is probable but that it is highly probable. Clear and convincing proof must be strong and compelling proof, not merely proof that the existence of a fact is more likely than not. On the other hand, it is not as high a standard as the prosecutor must meet in a criminal case, where a criminal defendant may not be convicted unless the jury finds him guilty beyond a reasonable doubt. You should understand these words as carrying their everyday meaning. You may find for plaintiff only if his proof is *clear and convincing.*

IV. Elements 1 and 2 — Defamatory — Of and Concerning

The first two elements concern the message communicated by the CBS broadcast and should be considered together. I will first state them in a single sentence. *Plaintiff must prove that the broadcast contained a statement or message of defamatory meaning — about plaintiff personal-*

ly. The first element is that the message must have had a *defamatory meaning*; the second is that it must have been *about General Westmoreland personally*.

Plaintiff must prove these two elements by a preponderance of the evidence.

A. I will first discuss what is meant by "defamatory."

1. Not every critical or uncomplimentary statement is considered defamatory under law. To be defamatory, the statement must convey a message that exposes a person to contempt, hatred or ridicule; that harms a person's reputation, or lowers him in the estimation of a substantial part of the community.

An assertion that is merely unpleasant, offensive or embarrassing or merely hurts someone's feelings is not defamatory.

2. Second, in order to be defamatory, the statement must communicate some fact about the person. It is not sufficient if it asserts a low opinion of the person. For example, if a newspaper or program said of me that I was a lazy or stupid judge or that my decisions were foolish or irresponsible, that would not be a defamation; I could not base a lawsuit on it. If on the other hand it said that I had taken a bribe, or had decided cases based on whether the lawyers were my friends, that would be accusing me of bad facts. It would be a defamatory statement and could be the basis of a lawsuit for defamation.

B. *Of and Concerning.* As the second element plaintiff must prove, also by a preponderance of the evidence, that the defamatory statement of the broadcast was, in the words of the law, *of and concerning* him. This means that the defamatory message must have been a message about General Westmoreland personally.

It would not be sufficient if the statement accused a group of which the plaintiff was a member. For example, it would not be sufficient if the broadcast accused the military, the Army, MACV or military intelligence. Nor would a statement be defamatory of the plaintiff merely because it accused officers for whom he was responsible as their commander. The defamatory statement must be made about the plaintiff personally for him to prevail on this issue.

C. *What Plaintiff Claims Were the Defamatory Statements About Him.* In bringing this lawsuit, plaintiff has identified what he contends were the defamatory messages about him. You must decide whether the broadcast made any of these assertions about plaintiff.

Plaintiff contends the assertions made about him are the following: I will refer to them as the Alleged Libels.

1. In the year leading up the Tet Offensive, General Westmoreland engaged in a conscious effort to suppress, alter and conceal from his military and civilian superiors critical intelligence on the size of the enemy.

2. In the period from spring to fall of 1967, General Westmoreland willfully and improperly blocked intelligence and evidence on the size of the enemy from being communicated to his superiors.

3. General Westmoreland suppressed and concealed from his superiors that, in addition to the infiltrators his command had reported, he believed that an additional 100,000 to 150,000 North Vietnamese soldiers had infiltrated into South Vietnam in the months of September 1967 through January 1968.

4. During the months following the Tet Offensive, General Westmoreland engaged in a conscious effort to conceal from his military and civilian superiors critical intelligence on the size of the enemy force.

You must limit your inquiry to the Alleged Libels. As to each of these, you are to answer the question whether the broadcast made this assertion and whether it made the assertion about the plaintiff personally.

Statements in the broadcast accusing General Westmoreland of deceiving the Congress, the press and the American public, cannot be the basis of your finding that the broadcast was defamatory because they are not among the Alleged Libels. They are not what the lawsuit is about. Plaintiff has alleged only accusations that he tried to deceive the President and his military commanders. You may find defamatory content only if you find this message in the broadcast.

D. *How to Decide.* To determine whether the broadcast conveyed any of the messages plaintiff alleges and whether they were defamatory, you are to consider how the average television viewer would have understood the broadcast.

You are to decide this in the context of the broadcast as a whole, including the words, the inflection with which they were spoken, the expressions of speakers, the pictures, the sound — in short, everything about the broadcast. You may consider also the advertising and prior publicity by CBS about the broadcast in deciding how the average viewer would have understood it.

You should of course consider the literal meaning of the words used in the documentary. But plaintiff is not required to prove that the words in their literal meaning defamed him. Nor is he required to point to any specified sentence or paragraph that states the allegedly defamatory accusation. You must consider the entire broadcast, and you should consider whether it makes these accusations *by inference* as well as by explicit statement. Plaintiff is not required to convince you that every single viewer would have so understood the broadcast to make the accusation.

Plaintiff prevails on this issue if you find that the average viewer, watching and listening to the program as a whole, would have understood it to convey the defamatory message about him that he has alleged.

E. If a statement or message about the plaintiff has a defamatory meaning, it may be the basis of a libel suit even though the broadcaster was merely quoting, repeating or broadcasting what someone else had said. The accurate repetition of someone else's defamatory statement is a libel if plaintiff proves all the elements of libel, including that the defendants broadcast it believing it to be false or with reckless disregard whether it was false.

On your verdict form, you have a list of plaintiff's Alleged Libels. As to each Alleged Libel, you will answer whether you find that the documentary made that statement about plaintiff and whether it was defamatory. Your consideration of the other elements of truth/falsity, the defendants' state of mind, and damages will deal only with those alleged defamatory statements that you find were made by the broadcast about plaintiff.

V. *Third Element — Truth or Falsity of the Broadcast*

(a) As the third element, plaintiff must prove that at least one Alleged Libel made by the broadcast about him was false.

(b) As I have explained to you plaintiff must prove the falsity of defamatory statements by clear and convincing evidence. It is not sufficient, as with the first two elements, for him to prove falsity by a preponderance of the evidence — which means only that you find plaintiff's position more likely than not. You must find that plaintiff has demonstrated falsity by clear and convincing evidence.

Although we sometimes discuss this as the issue of *truth-or*-falsity, you must remember that there is no burden on defendants to convince you of the truth of the broadcast. The defendants are free to offer proof of the truth of their broadcast, but by doing so they do not assume the burden of convincing you. The burden remains on plaintiff to convince you it is false.

(c) The issue of truth/falsity arises for each specified defamatory statement about plaintiff that you find was made by the broadcast. Plaintiff cannot prevail by proving falsity in other aspects of the broadcast. He is entitled to prevail on the issue of falsity if he proves that one specified defamatory statement made about in the broadcast was false.

(d) To prove falsity, plaintiff must prove that a defamatory statement was false in a significant way. If the statement is substantially true, the plaintiff has failed to prove its falsity, even though he may have proved it false in insignificant details.

How do you tell whether falsity is significant or insignificant? To help you make this distinction, you should think about the gist, or the sting of the particular defamatory statement. What is it about the statement that makes it defamatory? What aspect of the statement brings contempt, scorn, hatred or ridicule on plaintiff or lowers his estimation in the eyes of the community? That aspect of the statement can be described as its gist or sting. The statement must be false as to this aspect of the statement for plaintiff to have proved substantial falsity.

Let me give you a crude illustration. Suppose a newspaper writes of me that in 1983 together with Jones and Smith, and armed with a .45 revolver, I robbed a branch of the Chemical Bank on Broadway. I bring a libel suit. The jury finds that I did indeed rob a bank, but the other facts in the story were inaccurate: It was in 1982, not 1983; my colleagues were Harris and Thomas, not Jones and Smith; I was armed with a .38 and not a .45; it was the Chase and not the Chemical; it was on 3rd Avenue, not on Broadway. I suggest the jury might properly find that although I had proved falsity in many insignificant details, I had not proven significant falsity. As to the aspect of the newspaper story that was defamatory — the gist or sting of the libel — the accusation that I robbed a bank — *that part was true.* The defamatory statement was therefore substantially ture. The details found to be untrue were insignificant. They did not contribute in any important way to the defamatory nature of the statement. They were not the gist or sting of the libel.

In this case, I suggest to you that the gist of the defamatory statements alleged by plaintiff centers on the charge of General Westmoreland's dishonesty or bad faith in orders given and positions taken by him concerning the reporting of enemy strength in an effort to deceive the President and the plaintiff's superiors in the chain of command. If you find that plaintiff was the subject of defamatory statements as he has alleged, in order to prove substantial falsity of those statements plaintiff would have to prove to you that his positions were taken honestly and in good faith and that he made no effort to misrepresent the strength or capability of the enemy to the President or his superiors.

(e)(i) The issue of truth/falsity relates to plaintiff's own honesty, not to the honesty or dishonesty of other persons. To prove falsity, plaintiff would have to convince you that his actions were honest. It would not be sufficient for him to prove that the broadcast was wrong in charging that other persons had engaged in dishonest acts.

(e)(ii) The question of honesty or dishonesty is central. The question of the accuracy or inaccuracy of the positions taken and reported by MACV also plays a role in your consideration of the truth or falsity of the broadcast, but it is a somewhat tricky issue, which I want to go over with care.

If plaintiff has proved to you that his reports and positions were correct, then you would undoubtedly conclude also that he had acted honestly and in good faith in making those correct reports and you would find for plaintiff on the issue of the falsity of the broadcast.

If, however, you find that the MACV positions were wrong, the significance of that conclusion is more complicated.

Plaintiff can nonetheless prevail on the falsity issue. If he proves to you by clear and convincing evidence that, although inaccurate, his positions represented an honest, good faith effort to interpret the available evidence as accurately as possible, then you would find accusations of dishonesty to be false.

But, inaccuracy in General Westmoreland's positions can also support the conclusion that he did not honestly believe in those positions. It would be relevant how extreme you found the inaccuracy of his positions to be and how clearly the intelligence information available at the time showed this inaccuracy. If the inaccuracy was clear and extreme, this could lead you to conclude that General Westmoreland did not believe in his reported figures and acted dishonestly. If the information was cloudy and subject to differing interpretations and if the differences were slight, you might find that these were honest differences of opinion.

Thus you may consider the accuracy or inaccuracy of plaintiff's reports and positions as evidence, but the issue you must decide is whether plaintiff was acting honestly or dishonestly.

General Westmoreland has the burden of convincing you of his honesty.

(f) Next I want to discuss the relevance to the issue of truth/falsity of acts done by General Westmoreland's subordinates. The CBS broadcast spoke of widespread acts of falsification at lower levels in military intelligence functions relating to the Vietnamese Communist force strength. You have heard evidence from CBS witnesses stating that such falsification occurred. From plaintiff's witnesses you have heard denials that any such thing took place. It is for you to decide what the facts are. But your decision on this question is not necessarily determinative on the overall issue of the truth or falsity of the broadcast.

For the central issue, I say once again, relates to the honesty or dishonesty of General Westmoreland's acts and statements, not to those of his subordinates. The honesty or dishonesty of the acts of his subordinates may have significant bearing on your findings as to plaintiff's own honesty but not necessarily.

If you find that the broadcast was wrong and that no such acts of falsification occurred at lower levels, that would of course tend to support plaintiff's position but it does not conclude the question. The question remains for you to decide whether the statements made, reports issued and positions taken by the plaintiff were honest or dishonest. If General Westmoreland has failed to convince you of his honesty and his good-faith belief in the positions he took, then you would find for the defendants on the issue of truth, even though you might find that the broadcast was wrong as to specific acts of falsification done at lower levels.

If you find that acts of falsification did occur at lower levels as the CBS documentary stated, that would of course tend to support defendants' position, but it does not conclude the question. Two questions would be significant: Whether General Westmoreland was aware of and tolerated those acts of falsifications and whether those acts were done to support dishonest positions taken by General Westmoreland. Even if dishonest acts were done at lower levels, and even if they were done to carry out General Westmoreland's command position, General Westmoreland could nonetheless prevail on the falsity issue if he has proved to you (i) that he was unaware of such dishonest acts and (ii) that his command positions honestly represented his best beliefs.

But he must prove both of these: (1) if he was aware of false actions or of orders to block or falsify reports at lower levels and tolerated them, he cannot prove to you that he acted honestly with respect to intelligence. You would want to consider how likely it was that such actions could have occurred without General Westmoreland being aware of them. Your findings on this might be influenced by your conclusions as to how frequently such actions occurred, why did they occur, how extreme was their effect, and at how high a level did they occur.

(2) If you find that such false actions occurred at lower levels, General Westmoreland must prove more than that he was not aware of them to prevail on the truth issue. He must prove also that dishonest actions at lower levels were not in response to dishonest positions established by him. In other words, if General Westmoreland established positions that were not honest and did not represent his good faith beliefs, he cannot prove falsity of the broadcast just because he did not see what was done at lower levels to support his dishonest positions.

(g) The broadcast did not charge General Westmoreland with having personally participated in lower level details of falsification, such as cutting the reported strength of individual units, blocking lower level reports of infiltration or altering the computer data base after Tet. Accordingly, it is not an issue in the case whether General Westmoreland personally involved himself with such lower level falsifications and you could not find falsity based on your conclusion that General Westmoreland did not personally do these things. The issue is, in the things he did do — the orders he gave, and the positions he took — was he acting honestly or dishonestly?

(h) I have gone on at considerable length about the issue of truth/falsity because it includes some rather tricky questions on which I felt you could use some guidance. But the gist of the issue can be summed up in a nutshell. The question is whether General Westmoreland acted honestly or dishonestly with respect to the enemy strength in informing the President and his superiors.

(i) You may consider on the issue of the truth or falsity of the broadcast only the evidence that was received on that element. You may not consider evidence that was received solely on the defendants' state of mind, or on the issue of damage to General Westmoreland's reputation.

VI. 4th Element ——— Defendants' State of Mind

A. The fourth element that plaintiff must prove is the one we have referred to as the Defendants' State of Mind. Plaintiff must prove it by clear and convincing evidence. It deals with the defendants' belief about their broadcast. As to any defamatory statement made about him by the defendants' broadcast, it is not sufficient for the plaintiff to prove that it was false; he must prove in addition that a defendant either knew it was false or published it with reckless disregard as to whether it was false.

Now what does this mean?

a) The first branch — knowing falsity — is easy enough to understand. It means more or less the same thing as telling a lie. This standard would be satisfied if a defendant either knew or believed the statement to be false when he published it.

b) The second branch — recklessness — is more complicated. It does not mean exactly what you might mean when you use the word recklessness in everyday speech. It refers to a special situation.

The reckless state of mind is shown if a defendant recognized that the statement was probably false but went ahead and published it ignoring or disregarding the probability of falsehood.

Whenever I have spoken throughout the trial, or speak in these instructions, of the "recklessness" component, this is what I mean. I generally use a shorthand to refer to it, because it is too long to say in full every time. But each time I refer to it, whether I say "reckless falsity," "reckless disregard," "recognition of

probable falsity," or some other identifier, I am referring to this standard.
I will repeat it for you.

[Repeat]

The test of recklessness, like the test of knowing falsity, concentrates on the defendants' beliefs about the truth or falsity of their broadcast.

Recklessness is not made out by showing that defendants acted carelessly, negligently or sloppily in making the documentary. It is not made out by showing that defendants did not do a perfect job; or by your finding that factual errors occurred; it is not made out by showing that a more prudent or more reasonable reporter would have exercised greater care to avoid errors or by showing that defendants were unfair to General Westmoreland. Even if defendants did not act as reasonably prudent reporters or editors should, that is not sufficient to establish the reckless disregard or prohibited state of mind.

The test is essentially subjective. The question is not what others might have thought about defendants' acts, or what you think. It does not look to whether the defendants acted reasonably in making the documentary. It does not look to whether other reports or producers would have believed the defamatory statements or whether you the jurors would have believed them.

It looks at the defendants' beliefs. As to each defendant, it asks whether he recognized a probability that the defamatory statements about the plaintiff were false but when ahead disregarding it.

* * *

B. (i) As to the first three elements that dealt with the meaning of the broadcast and its truthfulness or falsity, whatever answer you reached was the same for each defendant. The issue of the defendants' state of mind is different. It examines the state of mind of each defendant and you must answer the question separately for each defendant. For each defendant and as to each false defamatory statement you find, you must answer whether that defendant had the prohibited state of mind.

How do you answer that question for the defendant CBS, which is a corporation and does not have a state of mind. To determine this as to CBS, you look at the beliefs of the person CBS charged with responsibility for the content of the broadcast. If you find that any of them had the prohibited state of mind, then you will find that CBS did also. If none of them did, then CBS did not, even though other CBS employees (who were not responsible for the content of the broadcast) might have believed the broadcast was false. Defendant CBS is answerable for the state of mind of any particular person to whom CBS gave responsibility for the content of the broadcast.

The persons who had responsibility for the content of the broadcast are George Crile — the producer, Mike Wallace — the correspondent, Sam Adams — the consultant, Joe Zigman — the Associate Producer, Howard Stringer — the Executive Producer, Andrew Lack — the senior producer, and Roger Colloff — then Vice President and Director of Public Affairs.

CBS may be found liable only if you find that one of those persons proceeded with the prohibited state of mind.

If that state of mind has not been established as to one of those persons, it cannot be attributed to CBS.

As to each individual defendant, Mr. Wallace, Mr. Adams and Mr. Crile, you must consider his state of mind separately. In order to find any one of them liable you must find that he personally had the forbidden state of mind. You may not find any one of them liable by reason of the state of mind of another person. You may not find any of them liable because you found CBS to be liable.

(ii) I want to emphasize that the element of the defendants' state of mind refers to their beliefs *at the time of the broadcast (1/23/82)*, not earlier or later. If you found that a defendant doubted the truth of the broadcast's message at an early stage of its production, that would not be a basis for holding the defendant liable — if by the time it was aired he had become convinced it was true. Nor would it matter that a defendant or a responsible CBS employee developed doubts after the broadcast. If you have heard evidence of disbelief or doubt by any of them at an earlier or later stage, you may consider it only to help you decide whether they disbelieved or substantially doubted the truth of the broadcast at the time of its airing.

(iii) In deciding whether any defendant disbelieved or recognized a probability of falsity of the broadcast you should consider all the evidence that has been received on the defendants' state of mind.

This includes what was told to Mr. Adams, Mr. Crile and Mr. Wallace by the persons they interviewed — both on camera and off camera. [It includes statements of persons who agreed with the broadcast thesis and those who did not.] It includes the documents the defendants read dating from the 1967–68 period and includes also books and reports they read dating from a later time commenting on military intelligence in that period.

You may consider whether all of this did or did not support what the defendants put in the broadcast, remembering however that the question is not whether you would have relied on and believed it, but whether the defendants did.

If the defendants genuinely believed what they put in the broadcast, it makes no difference whether you would have drawn the same conclusions from the materials defendants found from their research.

On the other hand, if a defendant had the prohibited state of mind of knowing or reckless falsity, you must find for plaitniff on this issue even though the defendants' research may have included documents or interviews that supported the broadcast.

I told you earlier that the defendant could commit a libel merely by repeating accurately a defamatory statement made by someone else. If you find that the defendants' broadcast repeated a false defamatory statement about plaintiff made by someone else, you must evaluate the state of mind with which defendants included the accusation.

It is of course proper for reporters to interview others in researching their stories. That is an important way for them to get information. If the reporter or editor or broadcasting company publishes such a defamatory statement and it is found by you to be false, you must decide whether it was published by the defendants with the knowledge that it was false or whether the defendants recognized that it was probably false, and published it anyway disregarding that probability. If plaintiff has proved that then plaintiff has proved this element.

If on the other hand the defendants believed the truth of the source's statement in broadcasting it, the defendants have not committed any offense even though the source may have deceived the defendants by deliberately lying.

(iv) I emphasize again that it is not the defendants' reasonableness that is at issue but rather their beliefs.

* * *

C. *Problem Issues*

I want to discuss with you certain categories of evidence — not because they are more important or less important than any other category — but because they could lead you to confusion. I discuss them only to avoid such confusion because these categories of evidence may be considered in certain ways but not in others. These types of evidence have relevance, but they are not determinative.

(1) *Thoroughness of Research*

First, the thoroughness of the defendants' research. You may of course consider thoroughness. Defendants argue that they did a very thorough job interviewing some 80 witnesses and consulting thousands of documents over months of preparation. Plaintiff argues that defendants decided what they wanted to say at the outset and were thorough in interviewing witnesses who would support their thesis but didn't speak to significant witnesses who have contradicted it.

You may consider both of these arguments but only insofar as they bear on the issue of knowing or reckless falsity.

You are not to put yourselves in the position of the television editor or critic deciding whether the research was or was not sufficiently thorough. There is no obligation in the libel law to acquire the strongest evidence through the most careful research. The legal obligation is that a defendant may not broadcast with knowing or reckless falsity, as I have explained to you.

If you find that CBS failed to interview a witness who would have been important, this could affect your finding *on defendants' state of mind* if you find that a defendant disbelieved or recognized probably falsity of the broadcast and deliberately avoided the witness so as not to receive information that would show it to be wrong.

But if the plaintiff has failed to show disbelief, or recognition of probable falsity on the defendants' part, you may not find for the plaintiff merely because you think in fairness or in the interests of better journalism they should have sought out such witnesses.

If you find that defendants had sources they believed to be reliable and truthful

Appendix 2 — Westmoreland Proposed Jury Instructions

and relied on these sources in publishing, then they did not act with the forbidden state of mind, even if you think that a more thorough investigation might have prevented error in the broadcast or that you yourselves would not have believed the defendants' sources.

(2) *Reliability of Sources*

You may consider whether the sources the defendants claim to have relied on in making their broadcast were reliable or not, but only to help you decide whether you find that defendants in fact believed and relied on those sources. If you find those sources to be of such little value that you do not believe the defendants' claims that they relied on those sources, you might then find that the defendants disbelieved their broadcast or recognized a probability that it was false. If, on the other hand, you believe the defendants' claim that they believed and relied on those sources, it is of no significance that you might think they shouldn't have relied on them.

(3) *Bias, Ill-Will, Toward Plaintiff*

Plaintiff contends the defendants were biased against him. If you find this is true, it is relevant evidence only for limited purposes. If you find the defendants had a bias, or harbored ill-will toward the plaintiff, you may consider whether such ill will led the defendants to publish defamatory statements they knew were false or as to which they recognized a probability they were false. If defendants did so, plaintiff has proved the prohibited state of mind.

But if plaintiff has failed to prove that defendants published false statements knowingly or with reckless disregard, then it would make no difference that a defendant was biased against the plaintiff.

(4) *Previously Formed Belief*

Plaintiff contends also that the defendants started on their investigation with an already fixed premise and conducted their investigation with a closed mind seeking only such evidence as would confirm their premise. If you find this to be true, you may consider it in determining whether defendants made the broadcast with the prohibited state of mind. If you find that defendants' commitment to a previously adopted premise led them to broadcast things they had learned were not true or led them to proceed recklessly disregarding the recognized probable falsity of their broadcast, plaintiff has proved that defendants had the prohibited state of mind.

On the other hand, you may not find for the plaintiff on this issue only because you find that defendants' mind was made up already at the start of the investigation. It is normal that reporters investigate where their suspicions or beliefs lie. If the defendants believed in the truth of their documentary at the time it was broadcast, the law of libel is not violated by the fact that they formed the belief long before.

(5) *Fairness of the Broadcast*

Plaintiff contends the broadcast was unfair in several respects. You may consider this contention insofar as it helps you decide the issue of defendants' state of mind. If you find unfairness in defendants conduct in making the broadcast or in the finished product, it may be evidence of bias which in turn you may consider in deciding whether the defendants were motivated by such bias to publish with knowing or reckless falsity. Also you may consider whether any unfairness involved the publication of material known to be false or the reckless publication of material recognized as probably false If so, plaintiff has proved the element.

But you must recognize that unfairness or onesidedness does not in itself establish the prohibited state of mind.

Under the libel law, there is no obligation to be fair or to present both sides of the story.

When a newspaper, book or broadcast comments on the actions of a public official, as long as it acts honestly in good faith by not publishing false matter knowingly or in reckless disregard of a recognized probably falsity, it has no obligation under the libel law to act fairly, present both sides, seek out witnesses favoring the other side, give equal advantage to witnesses on the other side or even publish their statements. There is no legal obligation even to interview the subject of its criticism. How a broadcaster chooses to act in these respects is a matter of its editorial policy; in these matters it is free to act in whatever manner it thinks best.

Recognizing the importance of free and open discussion in the press of the actions of public officials, the law of libel imposes no obligations of fairness or evenhandedness on the press. The publication of commentary that flatly accuses public officials of bad and dishonest acts, without including their denials or the evidence to the contrary, is a daily event. Each of us is entitled to our own opinion whether this a good or bad thing. But your opinion on that subject may not enter into your deliberations as jurors.

You may not act in the role of super editor or TV critic and base your decision on whether you think the broadcast would have been better or fairer if it had been investigated or presented in a different manner.

The libel law concerns itself with truth and honesty, not with fairness. The obligation under the libel law is not to publish false defamatory matter knowingly or in reckless disregard of probable falsity. You may consider factors of unfairness only to the extent they support a finding of knowing or reckless falsity. The issue you are to decide is whether the plaintiff has shown such knowing or reckless falsity.

(6) *Tone of Questioning*

Plaintiff contends the defendants used a friendly and encouraging tone in questioning witnesses who supported the thesis of the broadcast but used a harsh accusatory tone with General Westmoreland and the witnesses who supported him.

You may properly consider this contention on the issue of defendants' state of mind. If you find that the tone and manner of the questioning were used by defendants to prevent adverse witnesses from bringing out the truth, this would be evidence supporting a finding of the prohibited state of mind. If you find the tone of questioning showed bias on the part of defendants, you may consider that in the manner I explained earlier.

You must recognize on the other hand that using a harsh tone in questioning is not prohibited by the libel law. The use of a harsh questioning tone is a proper journalistic technique, [just as it is a proper technique for a lawyer conducting a cross examination.(?)] It may be useful to bring out the truth. It can also be used to create confusion or conceal the truth.

You may consider the tone of questioning in deciding whether the defendants broadcast false matter knowingly or in reckless disregard of its probable falsity. But a hostile tone of questioning is not a sufficient basis for finding the prohibited state of mind.

(7) *Editing*

Plaintiff contends that in defendants' editing of the interviews, the writing of the narrative portions and the construction of the broadcast, defendants created misleading distortions. You may properly consider such contentions and such evidence, insofar as they support proof of the prohibited state of mind.

Editing is a proper and necessary part of news or commentary. When a witness has been interviewed at length, editing is necessary if a quotation is to be presented without broadcasting the entire interview. A broadcaster has considerable latitude to edit such material in whatever manner he thinks best, and cannot be found to have acted with improper state of mind merely because the jury disagrees with the manner with which the editing selection was made. If the editing produces a fair account of the views the witness expressed, there would be no prohibited state of mind even though the editing might have changed substantially a particular sentence spoken by the witness.

On the other hand, if a broadcaster in the course of editing so distorts the material as to present a false account of the witness' views and gives false support to the broadcasts' accusation, this could amount to publication of knowingly false defamatory material. The question once again is not whether you like or dislike the editing process generally or the editing done on this documentary. The question is whether defendants broadcast defamatory material they knew to be false or broadcast it recklessly despite recognition of probable falsity.

* * *

I have discussed these arguments with you not to increase or to lessen their importance. How much importance you attach to those kinds of proof is for you alone to decide. I have discussed them only to avoid confusion — to be sure that you consider them only for their proper purposes under the libel law.

VII. *Deliberations, Exhibits and Questionnaire*

A. *Order of Deliberations*

You will deal with the elements I have explained one by one, reaching a verdict on each element before proceeding to deliberate on the next. You will deal with them in the same order that I have followed in explaining them. I have prepared a questionnaire which sets forth in order the questions you must answer. In a few moments I will go over the questionnaire in detail.

B. *Exhibits*

It is most important that, in considering each element, you use only the evi-

Appendix 2 — Westmoreland Proposed Jury Instructions

dence that has been admitted on that element. When you consider the question of the truth or falsity of the broadcast, you will use only the evidence received on that issue and will consider evidence received on the issue of the defendants' state of mind, or on the damage to the plaintiff's reputation. And when you move on to consider the defendants' state of mind, again you will use only the evidence received on that issue and will not consider evidence admitted on truth, or other questions.

We have arranged several devices to help you follow this instruction.

First, you will be given a master list of the exhibits which tells you next to each identifying number what the exhibit is and, in the right hand column, what is the element of which the exhibit is received. This master list has been divided into separate lists which will be given to you. One is labeled Truth/Falsity; it includes the exhibits on that issue. A second is labeled Defendants' State of Mind which lists all the exhibits received on that issue.

Also, the exhibits will be divided into separate boxes. One box will be labeled Truth/Falsity. When you deliberate on that issue you will use only the exhibits in that box. When you have answered that question and move on to the issue of defendants' state of mind, you will put the *truth* exhibits back in their box and use only the exhibits contained in the box labeled Defendants' State of Mind.

Furthermore, each exhibit will be stamped on its face (at the upper left hand corner) to indicate the element to which it relates.

C. *Questionnaire*

Now please follow with me the questionnaire.

I. & II. The first section of the questionnaire is numbered I. & II. because it covers both the first and second elements. You will see listed here the four Alleged Libels that plaintiff contends were conveyed by the broadcast. As to each of the four, you will answer three questions:

  i. whether the broadcast conveyed this statement or message;

  ii. whether you find the message to be of defamatory meaning;

  iii. whether that defamatory message was *of and concerning* General Westmoreland.

When you have completed this part of the questionnaire, if you answered YES to all three questions for any one of the four Alleged Libels, you will then check the box showing you have found for plaintiff on that Alleged Libel. If you do not have three YES answers, you check the box indicating that you find for defendants on that Alleged Libel. If you find for plaintiff on any of the four Alleged Libels, you will send me a note through the marshal advising me simply that you have completed the questions for Elements I. & II., and will move on to consider Element III — truth or falsity.

If you do not find for plaintiff on any of the Alleged Libels, you should send a note advising of that fact and I will then give you further instructions.

III. You will then turn to the question whether plaintiff has proven the substantial falsity of defamatory statements made about him by the broadcast.

You will answer only as to Alleged Libels on which you found for plaintiff in Elements I and II. If you found for defendants on any of the Alleged Libels for Elements I and II, you need not answer any further questions on that Alleged Libels.

For any Alleged Libel, if plaintiff has proved to you that it was substantially false, you will check the line indicating that you find for the plaintiff. If plaintiff has failed to prove the substantial falsity, you will check the line showing that you find for the defendants.

When you have answered the questions on the form as to truth/falsity of the broadcast, you will send me a note through the marshal advising me simply that you have completed the questionnaire for the element of truth/falsity. You will not reveal in this note what decision you have reached.*

* The record will reflect that it was the joint request of the parties that the verdicts on truth and state of mind be announced simultaneously rather than separately when reached. The court would have preferred separate announcements as done in *Sharon v. Time Inc.*, but yields to the joint request of the parties.

IV. *Defendants' State of Mind*

After completing the questionnaire on truth/falsity, you will proceed to decide the issue whether the defendants broadcast their documentary with the prohibited state of mind.

On this issue you must answer separately as to each defendant. This form so provides. It lists the three individual defendants in alphabetical order and then lists CBS. You may consider the defendants in whichever order you choose, but remember that you find against CBS only if you find the prohibited state of mind on the part of one of the persons to whom CBS gave responsibility for the content of the broadcast, and you may find against an individual defendant only if you find that he personally acted with the prohibited state of mind.

Under the name of each defendant, the questionnaire states "On the question whether plaintiff has proved that the defendant acted with the prohibited state of mind, we find for plaintiff _____ (or) for the defendant _____."

For each Alleged Libel, you will check whether you find for plaintiff, or for the particular defendant.

When you have completed these questions, you will advise me by sending a note through the marshal that you have made your findings on the state of mind element.

At that point, I will call you into the court room to receive your findings on the first four elements.

APPENDIX 3

Westmoreland v. CBS

Judge Leval's Statement to the Jury

February 19, 1984

Members of the jury, we have been together a long time and have gotten to know each other a bit. It has been a privilege to be with you.

I have watched you with admiration. I have been impressed by your diligence, attentiveness and patience; and by your determination to do your job.

The jury system is an extraordinary thing. Juries are composed of men and women drawn at random from lists of citizens who are then given great responsibility and power.

We demand of them that they put aside bias, listen to the evidence and judge as fairly as they would wish to be judged. It is a tall order.

You have shown from the first that the job was in good hands.

The settlement of the action deprives you of the opportunity to render a verdict. I can understand if you feel a sense of letdown — a sense of disappointment.

Lest you be too disappointed, I suggest some thoughts on the other side.

We have been participants in a most interesting and unusual proceeding — a trial seeking the judgment of history.

There can be no such thing as legal power to fix the judgment of history. Such judgments must be left to study, reflection and debate.

We have watched the creation of an extraordinary, unique and rich record for historians to study. I suggest that the value of the proceeding may have more to do with the record it has created for history than with the verdict it can produce.

Judgments of history are too subtle and too complex to be resolved satisfactorily with the simplicity of a verdict — such as, we find for the plaintiff, we find for the defendant.

Also they are too subject to debate and disagreement to be resolved by an constituted authority.

I think it is safe to say that no verdict either you or I would be able to render could escape widespread disagreement.

So I suggest to you it may be for the best that this verdict will be left to history.

As for your conduct, you have earned the gratitude and admiration of the court, the parties, and the lawyers.

We are indebted to counsel on both sides for the remarkable job they have done placing this case before us. I don't know whether you can imagine how much work has gone into the preparation of this case over nearly three years.

For both sides, the evidence has been presented with skill, forcefulness and total command of the voluminous materials.

The positions of counsel were presented with dignity, as well as force. We can be confident that historians who study this record will find it fully and clearly developed.

APPENDIX 4
Sharon v. Time
Jury Instructions

Ladies and gentlemen, when this trial began I asked you to pay close attention to the evidence. I am grateful that, throughout this long and complicated case, you have given everything that happened your sober attention. Your duty now is to decide the facts. I will instruct you on the law that you must apply, and you are bound by your oaths as jurors to follow my instructions, just as you must abide by all my rulings as to what evidence you may consider, and on what issue or issues. But as to the issues of fact, your decisions will be final. You must pass on the weight of the evidence and the credibility of the witnesses. You must decide who was telling the truth and who was not. You must discuss the contested events and decide as a group what was said and what occurred.

It is your recollection of what was said by the witnesses that is controlling — not any comments of the lawyers, not any of my comments. You must give no evidentiary weight to any comments or unanswered questions by the attorneys, and you must entirely disregard any comments that I may have made in ruling on objections or at any other time. Do not be misled into thinking from any comment I made, or from any question I asked, that I hold any view on the factual issues in this case. I am entirely neutral on all the factual issues. It is your judgment on the facts, and yours alone, that counts.

This case must be considered and decided by you as an action between persons of equal standing in the community. Time Incorporated, as a corporation, is entitled to the same fair trial at your hands as is an individual or a government official. A corporation is only a group of persons treated by the law as if it were an individual having rights or liabilities distinct from those of the persons composing it. Similarly, a famous public official, like plaintiff, is entitled to be treated fairly by you. He is to be given no special consideration or disadvantage because he is a foreigner; Congress has authorized him to sue in this court, and he must be treated like any other party. All persons and companies stand equal before the law and are to be dealt with as equals in this court of justice.

You will better understand the rules of law about which I am now informing you if you keep in mind that this case involves balancing of values, both of which are important in our society. Under certain conditions, the law of New York State grants plaintiffs the right to recover for false, defamatory statements which injure their reputations. The law in effect recognizes that the reputations of individuals are sometimes important enough to warrant legal protection from the injury that can be inflicted by false, defamatory statements. On the other hand, the law of New York and our federal constitution guarantee to individuals, and particularly to the press, freedom of speech. This constitutional guarantee entitles the press to publish critical statements about people, and protects the press from any liability for such statements, unless the statements are of such a nature and are made under such circumstances as to deprive those persons who make them of protection. In this case, the statements on which suit has been brought relate to a public official, and concern his official duties. The law affords the press particularly broad protection in these circumstances, in order to avoid inhibiting comment and debate. To recover even for a false, defamatory statement, a public official such as plaintiff must establish that the statement was made with "actual malice" — that is, with knowledge that the statement was false or with a reckless disregard for its truth or falsity.

In applying these principles of law that I give you, you must be concerned not only with the legal standards as such, but also with what the law calls the burden of proof. The plaintiff, Minister Sharon, has the burden of proving every disputed element of his claim against Time. Minister Sharon will have to prove one aspect of his claim by what the law calls a "preponderence of the evidence," and he will have to prove two aspects of his claim by what the law calls "clear and convincing evidence." If you conclude that Minister Sharon has failed to establish any aspect of his claim by whatever burden of proof applies, then you must decide the particular issue on which there has been a failure of proof against him. Before going any further I will define for you the two burdens of proof you are called upon to apply in this case.

What does "a preponderance of the evidence" mean? To establish a fact by a preponderance of the evidence means to prove that the fact is more likely true than not true. A preponderance of the evidence means the greater weight of the evidence. It refers to the quality and persuasiveness of the evidence, not to the number of witnesses or documents. In determining whether a claim has been proved by a preponderance of the evidence in the case, you may consider the relevant testimony of all witnesses, regardless of who may have called them, and all the relevant exhibits received in evidence, regardless of who may have produced them.

If you find that the credible evidence on a given issue is evenly divided between the parties, then you must decide that issue against the party having this burden of proof. That is because the party bearing this burden must prove more than simply equality of evidence — he must prove the element at issue by a preponderance. On the other hand, the party with this burden of proof need prove no more than a preponderance. So long as you find that the scales tip, however slightly, in favor of the party with this burden of proof — that what the party claims is more likely true than not true — then that element will have been proved by a preponderance of the evidence.

Plaintiff has a different and more demanding burden of proof than "preponderance of the evidence" on two elements of his claim. Plaintiff must demonstrate two elements of his claim — that any defamatory statement made was false, and that defendant acted with "actual malice" — by "clear and convincing" evidence. Clear and convincing evidence is a more exacting standard proof by a preponderance of the evidence. Clear and convincing proof leaves no substantial doubt in your mind. It is proof that establishes in your mind, not only that the proposition at issue is probable, but also that it is highly probable. This higher burden of proof is required by the Constitution to protect the rights enjoyed by the press and public to speak freely about public officials and their conduct. On the other hand, "clear and convincing" proof is not as high a standard as the burden of proof applied in criminal cases, which is proof "beyond a reasonable doubt." It is enough if plaintiff establishes falsity or actual malice beyond any "substantial" doubt; he does not have to dispel every "reasonable doubt."

You are by now familiar with the facts in this case. Plaintiff Ariel Sharon has one claim. He has sought to prove that a paragraph in the February 21, 1983 issue of Time Magazine libeled him. To establish this claim Minister Sharon must prove four essential elements:

First, that the challenged paragraph was defamatory of plaintiff in some actionable respect, as defined in these instructions;

Second, that any actionable defamatory statement contained in the challenged paragraph was false in some material respect;

Third, that Time published any actionable and false defamatory statement in the challenged paragraph with "actual malice," that is, that a responsible person or persons at Time published each such statement knowing it was false or seriously doubting its truth; and

Fourth, that any actionable and false defamatory statement contained in the paragraph in question and published with actual malice was the proximate cause of actual injury to plaintiff. You will be required to consider this fourth element separately only after you pass upon the first three elements of plaintiff's claim.

Defendant denies each and everyone of these elements. If you find that plaintiff has failed to establish any one of the elements of his claim, then it will be your duty to find for the defendant. Conversely, if you find that plaintiff has established all the elements of his claim, then it will be your duty to find for the plaintiff.

I. *DEFAMATORY MEANING*

The first element which plaintiff must prove is that a statement or statements in the paragraph of which he complains is "defamatory". A communication is defamatory if it tends to expose a person to hatred, ridicule or contempt — that is, if it tends to harm the reputation of that person so as to lower him in the estimation of the community or to deter others from associating or dealing with him. Not every unpleasant or uncomplimentary statement is defamatory. A publication that is unpleasant, offensive, or embarrassing, or that hurts the plaintiff's feelings, is not necessarily defamatory. To be defamatory a statement must tend to bring plaintiff into disrepute, or must tend to prejudice the plaintiff in the eyes of a substantial part of the community. In this connection, the relevant community for determining defamatory meaning in those reasonable or right-thinking readers of Time in the United States and abroad who read the Article at issue in the English language.

In reading the paragraph at issue, you must give its language a plain, natural, unstrained meaning, putting yourself in the position of the average reader. You need not determine that all of Time's readers interpreted the statements in a defamatory manner, but only that the average reader of Time Magazine would have understood the statements in a defamatory manner. You must also consider defendant's statements in their context, which in this case includes the Article as a whole, including its accompanying photographs, title and subtitle, as well as the Kahan Commission Report, to which the paragraph at issue refers. That inferences are to be drawn from the context of a statement does not diminish its force as a possible libel.

In addition to what is literally stated, you should consider what the statements imply. The words of the paragraph at issue, considered in the abstract, are not defamatory in their literal sense. The issue before you, however, is whether the same words, read in context, imply a defamatory meaning. The plaintiff contends that, in addition to what the statements in the allegedly offending paragraph literally say, they reasonably imply and were read by the average reader to state that, because of the discussion which the paragraph alleges to have occurred, Minister Sharon knew in advance that the Phalangists intended to take revenge against noncombatants at Sabra and Shatilla, but that he nevertheless told the Phalangists that he expected them to go into Sabra and Shatilla and take military action there. Plaintiff also contends that the paragraph implicitly states, by its reference to Appendix B of the Commission Report, that the Kahan Commission knew that plaintiff had discussed revenge with the Gemayels just before the massacre, and chose to keep that knowledge secret. Plaintiff claims that the statement that Appendix B contains details of the discussion described in the paragraph, when viewed in the context of the Commission's findings tending to exculpate plaintiff with regard to his intention and role in connection with the massacre, makes the "sting" of the paragraph more defamatory. The ultimate and combined effect of these statements, plaintiff argues, was to lead the average reader to conclude that plaintiff must have consciously intended to permit or actively encouraged the Phalangists to take acts of revenge against the noncombatant population in Sabra and Shatilla, extending to the deliberate killing of such noncombatants.

In determing whether the average reader would have read the defendant's statements as defamatory you are free to consider all the evidence relevant to this issue which has been admitted into the record. Thus, for example, you may consider the materials from which the allegedly offending paragraph was prepared, including the World Wide memo of December 6, 1982 (PX 8), the writing we have referred to as "Take 9" (PX 11), the drafts of the Article, and other evidence of what Time's personnel may have been attempting to communicate. In this connection you may consider whether the relevant Time employees thought the paragraph at issue was consistent with earlier materials; whether they thought it was innocuous or significant;

and the manner in which it was described in Time's press release (PX 25). Keep in mind that, though you may consider evidence of what the responsible Time employees intended to communicate in researching and writing the paragraph at various points prior to its publication, it is how the words actually used in the paragraph as published were understood, not how defendant intended that they be understood, that determines whether they are defamatory. Thus, for example, if the paragraph in context is not defamatory in at least one of the two ways required by these instructions, you must render a verdict for defendant even if you find, for example, that the World Wide Memo was defamatory in one of the ways required.

I am also permitting you to consider on this subject testimony and exhibits reflecting merely the fact that articles were published in newspapers, here and abroad, after Time's story was issued, and before Minister Sharon commenced suit. You must not consider this testimony or these articles, or any other articles, whether in English or in some foreign language, for the truth of what they state, or in determining how the average reader construed the paragraph at issue. But you may consider this evidence in determining the extent to which the paragraph at issue was referred to in newspapers, here and abroad, which you may find relevant in evaluating the claim of the defendant that the paragraph has only an "innocuous" meaning. Finally, while you may consider all the materials properly before you in determining whether plaintiff has proved by a preponderance of the evidence that the average reader would have given the paragraph at issue a defamatory meaning, you must decide ultimately whether the language of the paragraph itself, read in context, defamed plaintiff.

The issue of defamatory meaning is complicated in this case by the various degrees of culpability that are arguably implicit in the paragraph at issue. Culpability can be described in many ways, with many shades of meaning. You have heard many such descriptions during the trial, including such words as "condoned," or such phrases as "must have known in advance." You should not be concerned, however, with every conceivable degree of culpability, and all the possible descriptions. This is a lawsuit, and not a course in language or philosophy. The relevant issues here are narrowed by the surrounding factual circumstances, and by the claims that can fairly be said to have been presented by the complaint and the evidence. For present purposes you may find it helpful to consider the paragraph at issue as implicitly making one or more of the following statements to the average reader, keeping in mind that you are free to conclude that the paragraph contains none of these possible meanings:

1. Minister Sharon was *negligent*, in that he failed to exercise reasonable care under the circumstances to protect noncombatants;

2. Minister Sharon was *reckless*, in that he realized that substantial danger existed that noncombatants would be deliberately killed by the Phalangists, but unreasonably disregarded the danger in order to achieve other, legitimate ends;

3. Minister Sharon acted *knowingly*, in that, even though he did not consciously intend to allow the Phalangists to harm noncombatants, he was aware in advance that they were practically certain to engage in acts of revenge extending to the deliberate killing of noncombatants if he allowed them to operate in Sabra and Shatilla;

4. Minister Sharon acted with *subjective intent*, in that he consciously meant to allow the Phalangists to take revenge extending to the deliberate killing of noncombatants; and

5. Minister Sharon acted *purposefully*, in that he not only consciously intended to allow the Phalangists to take revenge extending to the deliberate killing of noncombatants in Sabra and Shatilla, but that he actively encouraged them to take such acts of revenge.

In principle, a statement imputing responsibility to a person for the deaths of noncombatants at any of these levels of culpability could support a claim of defamation. In determining whether the plaintiff in this case has proved that the paragraph made a defamatory statement or statements, however, you must keep in mind that, in the context of the Commission Report and in light of plaintiff's allegations, not every arguably defamatory meaning for the paragraph would establish an actionable defamation. This is essentially because the Commission Report explicitly made findings adverse to plaintiff on which Time had an absolute right to report. Thus, the Commission stated (P. 71):

It is our view that responsibility is to be imputed to the Minister of Defense for having disregarded the danger of acts of vengeance and bloodshed by the Phalangists against the population of the refugee camps, and having failed to take this danger into account when he decided to have the Phalangists enter the camps. In addition, responsibility is to be imputed to the Minister of Defense for not ordering appropriate measures for preventing or reducing the danger of massacre as a condition for the Phalangists' entry into the camps. These blunders constitute the non-fulfillment of a duty with which the Defense Minister was charged.

In addition, the Commission stated, on the question whether Minister Sharon in fact did consider the possibility that deliberate killings of noncombatants might occur in the camps (p. 68):

If, in fact, the Defense Minister, when he decided that the Phalangists would enter the camps without the IDF taking part in the operation, did not think that the decision could bring about the very disaster that in fact occurred, the only possible explanation for this is that he disregarded any apprehensions about what was to be expected because the advantages ... to be gained from the Phalangists' entry into the camps distracted him from the proper consideration in this instance....

Furthermore, Minister Sharon has not sued Time on the theory that it has merely rested the Commission's adverse findings; nor has he sued Time with respect to any of Time's views on the issues considered by the Commission. Rather, he has sued Time on the basis of only two defamatory means: that he consciously intended to permit the Phalangists to take acts of revenge extending to the deliberate killing of noncombatants; or that he actively encouraged the Phalangists to take revenge extending to the deliberate killing of noncombatants. Therefore, if you find that the only defamatory meanings in the allegedly offending paragraph are that Minister Sharon failed in his duty by disregarding the danger of acts of revenge extending to the deliberate killing of noncombatants, or that he must have considered the danger of such acts of revenge, or that the paragraph states only that plaintiff received an additional warning concerning the risk that acts of revenge would occur if the Phalangists were permitted to enter Sabra and Shatilla, or that, while he did not consciously intend to all the Phalangists to take revenge extending to the deliberate killing of noncombatants, he knew it was practically certain that such harm would occur if the Phalangists were allowed to operate in Sabra and Shatilla, then you must find the paragraph to be nondefamatory in the special circumstances of this case.

On the other hand, as you also know, the Commission made explicit findings tending to exonerate Minister Sharon in some respects. Among such explicit findings are the following (p. 51–52):

Contentions and accusations were advanced that even if IDF personnel had not shed the blood of the massacred, the entry of the Phalangists into the camps had been carried out with the prior knowledge that a massacre would be perpetrated there and with the intention that this should indeed take place; and therefore all those who had enabled the entry of the Phalangists into the camps should be regarded as accomplices to the acts of slaughter and sharing in direct responsibility. These accusations too are unfounded. We have no doubt that no conspiracy or plot was entered into between anyone from the Israeli polical echelon or from the military echelon in the IDF and the Phalangists, with the aim of perpetrating atrocities in the camps.

* * *

In having the Phalangists enter the camps, no intention existed on the party of anyone who acted on behalf of Israel to harm the non-combatant population, and ... the events that followed did not have the concurrence or assent of anyone from the political or civilian echelon who was active regarding the Phalangists' entry into the camps.

Plaintiff Sharon's claim in this case is that the paragraph in Time accuses him of having consciously intended to allow the Phalangists deliberately to kill non-combatants in Sabra and Shatilla, and of having actively encouraged such acts of revenge. I can tell you as a matter of law that any such statement, if you find it was made by the paragraph at issue, would constitute an actionable defamation of plaintiff for purposes of this case. Therefore, if you find that the paragraph states by implication that plaintiff consciously intended to allow the Phalangists deliberately to kill noncombatants, or that he actively encouraged such acts of revenge, then you should find the statement or statements involved to be defamatory.

In sum, if you find that the paragraph at issue, read in context, said only that Minister Sharon acted negligently or recklessly, or that, although he did not consciously intend to allow the Phalangists deliberately to kill noncombatants, he knew that such killings were practically certain to occur, then you should find that no actionable defamation was made by the paragraph at issue. On the other hand, if you find that the paragraph, read in context, states that Minister Sharon consciously intended to allow the Phalangists to engage in acts of revenge extending to the deliberate killing of noncombatants, or that he actively encouraged them to engage in such acts, then you must find that Time made an actionable, defamatory statement, and you should specify in your findings which statement or statements Time made. To the extent the Report's findings are relevant to your determination of this issue, it is ultimately for you to decide what the Commission found or did not find and what significance those findings may have in this case.

A final word on this subject is necessary with respect to the meaning of "revenge." You have heard, and you may consider, testimony about what "revenge" may have meant to various persons or groups. But ultimately you must decide this issue of defamatory meaning on how the average reader of Time would have understood "revenge" as it is used in the paragraph at issue. If you conclude that the average reader would have understood acts of revenge to mean only that the actual perpetrators of the murder of Bashir would be found and punished, or that terrorists in Sabra and Shatilla would be killed if they did not surrender, or that some innocent noncombatants would die as an inevitable consequence of the military operation that Minister Sharon contemplated, then the word "revenge" as used in the paragraph could not have conveyed a defamatory meaning. On the other hand, if you understand the statement in Time to mean, in context to the average reader, that Minister Sharon consciously intended to permit or encourage the Phalangists to commit, a limited number of murders or "atrocities" of noncombatants, as opposed to a full-scale massacre, those meanings would nevertheless be defamatory. If plaintiff shows that the average reader understood the paragraph to state that Minister Sharon consciously intended to allow or encouraged the Phalangists deliberately to kill innocent noncombatants for the purpose of revenge, and not as an inevitable result of the military operation contemplated, then the number or extent of the murders actually intended is irrelevant to the issue of defamatory meaning.

II. FALSITY

The second element which plaintiff must prove is the falsity of any defamatory statement that you find Time made. No matter how defamatory a statement may be, no matter what the defendant's motive in writing or publishing it, if the plaintiff fails to prove by clear and convincing evidence that the statement is false, you must render a verdict for the defendant.

The plaintiff must prove more than merely literal falsity. He must prove the falsity of the substance of the factual claims made in the paragraph at issue. In this case, therefore, plaintiff bears the burden of proving by clear and convincing evidence the falsity of the two separate facts which in context constitute the basis for the allegedly defamatory statements. Time has conceded the plaintiff has proved that Appendix B contains no mention of a discussion with the Gemayels or other Phalangists of the need to take revenge for Bashir's death. Plaintiff must therefore prove only that the discussion alleged in the Time paragraph did not occur. If you find that Minister Sharon actually had the discussion with the Gemayels described in the Article, then you must find for Time, even though Appendix B of the Report contains no details of such a discussion. Furthermore, plaintiff cannot prevail merely by proving that no discussion of revenge occurred at Bikfaya. If you find that credible evidence introduced at trial raises at least a reasonable possibility that plaintiff had a discussion with Phalangist leaders of the need to take revenge for the death of Bashir at the meeting at Karentina, during the morning of September 15, 1982 before he went to Bikfaya, then plaintiff must also prove that no such discussion occurred there. Similarly, if you find that the testimony raised a reasonable possibility that the minutes of the meetings at Bikfaya or Karentina provide support for defendant's paragraph, even though the Commission did not include details from the minutes in Appendix B, then plaintiff must clearly and convincingly disprove this possibility. Plaintiff has no burden to disprove these possibilities, however, unless you find that some credible evidence of their occurrence was presented. If you find that no such evidence was presented, plaintiff need only disprove the statements actually made in the paragraph.

The parties have placed before you their efforts to obtain information from the Government of Israel, and the results of those efforts. To the extent that admissible evidence has been obtained, and to the extent the parties have entered into stipulations as a result, you may consider such evidence and stipulations. The answers to the questions posed to Justice Kahan are the product of a process in which attorneys representing both parties participated, and were permitted to examine the underlying documents described in Justice Kahan's letter, including Appendix B and the minutes and reports of meetings represented by the Attorney General as having been obtained by the Commission. You have also been informed of types of materials which were not examined and of types of information which were not obtained, and you have been presented with the reservations of Time's attorney, Mr. Zadok. You should carefully evaluate whether, and if so the extent to which, the reservations stated by Mr. Zadok relate to the issue of falsity. Plaintiff has the burden of proof. Therefore, if plaintiff has failed to establish falsity by clear and convincing evidence, even if you feel that his failure is due to the parties' inability to obtain information from the Government of Israel, then you should render a verdict in defendant's favor. If, however, you find that plaintiff has met his burden of proof on falsity, through his own testimony, through the evidence actually obtained from Israel, through the testimony of Time personnel, and through the other evidence you may consider on this question, then you find for plaintiff even though some materials that might have been potentially useful evidence on this issue was not obtained from the Government of Israel or other sources.

One matter concerning the falsity issue warrants separate attention. Two witnesses from Time, David Halevy and Harry Kelly, testified at trial and during their depositions concerning their understanding of whether Minister Sharon testified publicly in October 1982, before the Commission that he had discussed revenge with the Gemayels. On the issue of falsity, all that matters is what you find Minister Sharon actually said before the Commission — the true meaning of his words — not what Halevy or Kelly may have believed about Sharon's testimony. If you believe that Sharon actually testified publicly that he discussed the need to take revenge for the death of Bashir with the Gemayels, then you may find on that basis alone that plaintiff has failed to prove falsity. If you find, however, that Sharon's public testimony referred to a discussion among Israelis about revenge, as you may find that Minister Sharon testified in this case, and as the linguist testified that Sharon's testimony must have been understood in Hebrew, then you should give no weight on the issue of falsity to any claimed understanding of Halevy and Kelly. Only if you reach the issue of actual malice will what Halevy and Kelly actually believed about Sharon's public testimony before the Commission become relevant.

In considering proof of falsity, you may also consider the plaintiff's testimony of what was discussed at Bikfaya and Karentina, as well as about what is contained in Appendix B of the Report. To the extent that your decision on this issue of falsity turns upon Minister Sharon's credibility, you should consider all the relevant evidence including his consistency, demeanor, bias, or interest in the outcome of this case, the minutes of the meetings and secret testimony examined by Justice Kahan and the attorneys, and the pssible evidence not examined by Justice Kahan. You may not consider Mr. Uri Dan's testimony on what was discussed at Bikfaya or Karentina, or on any other issue. But you should draw no inference whatever from the fact that I am not permitting you to consider his testimony. Finally, you must give no weight whatsoever on the issue of falsity to the testimony of Mr. Halevy as to what his sources told him about the meetings at issue, about the secret appendix, or about any minutes. What those sources might have said is not evidence of the truth of their statements, as they have not been identified, or placed under oath, or been made available for cross-examination. You may, however, consider Halevy's testimony as to his own observations at Bikfaya and in Lebanon generally immediately after Bashir's death, if you consider this testimony to be probative of whether Minister Sharon actually discussed the need for revenge with Phalangists during that period.

During this trial, I have permitted into evidence publications which Time personnel claim they read and considered in publishing the paragraph at issue. You may consider those articles as evidence of the truth of the fact at issue in this case (i.e., whether Minister Sharon discussed revenge with the Gemayels at Bikfaya). Even if a newspaper or magazine other than Time reported that Minister Sharon discussed with the Gemayels the need to take revenge for the death of Bashir, you cannot use that statement as evidence that proves to any extent or in any way that Minister Sharon in fact did have such a conversation. Nor may you consider those articles as evidence of the truth of any of the facts within the articles themselves. Thus, for example, articles that purport to describe meetings in which Minister Sharon participated cannot be relied upon in any way to prove or disprove that those meetings occurred as described. The reasons you may not consider such evidence on the question of truth or falsity are that the authors of the articles were not under oath when they wrote them, and the parties have had no opportunity to explore the basis for statements made in the articles, including the possible bias or unreliability of the writers or of the writer's sources. Those articles, in short, are not sufficiently reliable to be evidence on which you can properly rely for proof of truth or falsity, and it would be unfair and improper for you to do so.

Finally, ladies and gentlemen, keep in mind what Minister Sharon must prove: that he did not discuss the need to take revenge for the death of Bashir with the Gemayels at Bikfaya or with any Phalangists at any meeting after Bashir's death which the evidence suggests may have occurred. Minister Sharon is under no obligation to disprove other possible bases for a finding that he consciously intended to allow, or encouraged, the Phalangists to engage in acts of revenge in Sabra and Shatilla extending to the deliberate killing of noncombatants. The defendant withdrew its substantial truth defense when plaintiff made clear that he asserts only two defamatory meanings in this case. Time does not contend that it can prove the substantial truth of either of the defamatory meanings claimed.

Nevertheless, you heard considerable evidence of Minister Sharon's alleged motivations and culpability for the massacre, evidence that had no direct bearing on whether he had a discussion of the need to take revenge, as alleged in the Time paragraph. For example, defendant made an issue at this trial of the number of terrorists who actually stayed behind at Sabra and Shatilla, and the number of Phalangists sent into the camps to clear out the terrorists, thereby suggesting that plaintiff had no legitimate military motive in ordering the Phalangist operation. Similarly, defendant claimed that the discussions of revenge among the Israelis, the warnings received from some persons, the intimate contacts plaintiff had with the Phalangists, and the history of the Phalangist-Palestinian relations all rebutted plaintiff's claims that he did not consciously intend to allow and did not encourage the Phalangists deliberately to kill noncombatants in Sabra and Shatilla. This sort of evidence is properly before you, and the arguments of Time's attorney based on that evidence are logically relevant to the relatively narrow falsity issue that remains. But the manner in which this evidence may be considered is complex, and therefore is worth explaining in some detail.

First, general evidence of Minister Sharon's culpability, of the type just described, may be considered by you as potentially rebutting his proof of falsity. You may find that this evidence tends to prove, directly or indirectly, that Minister Sharon was more likely to have engaged in a discussion with Phalangists of the need to take revenge than if the evidence did not exist.

Second, you may consider any general evidence of culpability in evaluating the truthfulness of Minister Sharon's denial of having participated in a discussion of the sort alleged by Time. If you find that this general evidence of culpability establishes that Minister Sharon is not believable on any matters to which that evidence relates, you may tend to give less weight to his denials of having participated in a discussion about a need to avenge the death of Bashir.

In considering this sort of general evidence of culpability you should take into account all the relevant evidence on the issues involved. This includes the Commission Report's factual findings, and its inculpatory and exculpatory conclusions. Whether or not the sort of evidence of which I am speaking is worthy of your belief is for you to decide. You should not infer from my discussion of its possible relevance any judgment as to whether the evidence should be given any weight, and if so, how much. That is up to you. This discussion merely explains the proper basis upon which such evidence may be considered in deciding falsity, if you decide to give it weight one way or another.

Ultimately, you must only consider general evidence of culpability to the extent that you find it probative of the factual issue you must decide in rendering a verdict on falsity. You cannot simply speculate or guess, on the basis of unsupported suspicion or suggestions by counsel, that plaintiff must have had a discussion such as that alleged in Time's paragraph. You can use this sort of evidence to rebut plaintiff's proof only to the extent it actually tends to prove that he in fact had a discussion such as that alleged. Defendant has specifically declined the opportunity to prove the substantial truth of the alleged defamations in any manner other than by rebutting plaintiff's claim that he did not discuss the need for revenge.

III. *ACTUAL MALICE*

The third element which plaintiff must prove is that the defendant acted with "actual malice" in publishing the challenged paragraph. "Actual malice" means that the written statements were published with knowledge that they were false, or with reckless disregard for whether or not the statements were false. Plaintiff has the burden of proving actual malice by clear and convincing proof, as I have defined that term. Thus, your verdict must be for Time if plaintiff fails to prove his claim that the defendant, or any of its employees, acting in the course of their employment, actually knew that the challenged paragraph was untrue when published, or published the paragraph with a high degree of awareness that it was probably false. If, on the other hand, plaintiff proves actual malice by clear and convincing evidence, in any sufficient form, then your verdict must be for plaintiff on this issue.

In deciding the question of actual malice, or any other issue to which this point is relevant, keep in mind that the defendant is a corporation. A corporation can act only through its employees or other agents, and it is responsible for the acts of its employees and agents if those acts are performed within the scope of the employment or agency.

Actual malice is a legal term which you must not confuse with more common definitions of malice, such as ill will or hatred. Plaintiff cannot prevail merely by proving that the defendant was motivated by ill will, prejudice, hostility, hatred, contempt, or even a desire to injure. If you find that any of Time's employees was so motivated toward Sharon, you may consider such a state of mind as evidence that the employee might have published defamatory statements about Minister Sharon knowing they were false, or with a high degree of awareness of the likely falsity of such statements. But hostility, disapproval, or other forms of ill will do not as such establish actual malice; a reporter may despise someone but nevertheless publish only what he believes to be the truth in writing about that person. Therefore, while you may consider ill will or other relevant forms of bias, to prevail plaintiff must establish actual malice in the sense I have defined it.

The plaintiff can establish actual malice by proving, with respect to any false, defamatory statement you find, that Time published the statement with knowledge of its falsity, or with a reckless disregard for its truth or falsity. These two types of actual malice represent different degrees of awareness that an individual or individuals may have as to a statement's falsity.

Time is said to have acted with a reckless disregard for the truth of the statement if a person or persons at Time acted with a high degree of awareness as to the probable falsity of a statement. This is sufficient proof of actual malice even if no one at Time knew with certainty that the statement was false. On the other hand, reckless conduct is not measured by whether a reasonably prudent person would have published the statement involved. Your inquiry must ultimately be subjective — that is, you must find that a responsible employee of defendant in fact entertained serious doubts as to the truth of the publication. You may, however, find this subjective awareness of probable falsity, not only from direct proof as to the state of mind of defendant's employees, but also from the objective circumstances if you find from the evidence that obvious reasons existed to have led defendant's employees to doubt the accuracy of the statements published. In weighing these issues, you

Appendix 4 — Sharon Jury Instructions 33

may consider the behavior of all Time employees, including whether they investigated the facts in the paragraph, adequately questioned sources, or checked them with Minister Sharon before publication, so long as you remember that no duty to investigate or check exists beyond the duty to avoid publishing with actual malice. Conversely, you may consider whether Time employed measures for checking the accuracy of the paragraph at issue, including efforts to contact plaintiff for his comments prior to publication, which negate any inference that relevant Time employees sought to avoid learning the truth.

An important principle to keep in mind in deciding the issue of actual malice is that your decision must turn upon the state of mind of defendant and its responsible employees as of the time the alleged defamation was published. You may not rely on any evidence as to events or circumstances after publication, unless I permit you to consider such evidence because it pertains to credibility or to state of mind at the time of publication. In this connection, Time had no duty whatever after publication to investigate anyone's claim that the paragraph at issue was false, or to issue any retraction of the statements in the paragraph, or to check on whether Halevy's sources in fact exist or in fact gave him the information he claims to have received. You cannot consider any failure on Time's part to engage in these types of activities as probative of the existence of actual malice at the time of publication.

You may, however, consider two incidents that occurred after publication as possibly relating to credibility and to relevant state of mind prior to publication. First, you heard testimony that, very soon after publication of the paragraph, Mr. Olmert told Mr. Kelly that Appendix B contained no details of any discussion of revenge at Bikfaya; that Kelly expressed concern and asked Olmert to check on this statement; and that Olmert checked and reported back to Kelly. If you find that the evidence relating to this incident establishes that Kelly did not want to know the truth of the story he had authorized, you may also use this fact as evidence that Kelly may have seriously doubted the truth of the story before publication. On the other hand, you may choose to believe Kelly's version of these events, including his testimony that he did nothing with Olmert's information because Minister Sharon commenced suit against Time.

Second, you may consider, but only with respect to Halevy's credibility and state of mind, and only if you make the necessary preliminary findings which I will explain, the letter Halevy wrote to Duncan in May 1984 in which he states among other things his concerns with respect to Minister Sharon's "actual vindication." This letter can have no bearing whatever on the state of mind of any Time employee other than Halevy. Furthermore, you may consider the letter with respect to Halevy only if you find from other pre-publication evidence that the views expressed in the 1984 letter represent a continuing state of mind on Halevy's part, existing from some time prior to publication, as to Halevy's possible motives for knowingly reporting untrue facts about Minister Sharon, or for reporting facts with a high degree of awareness as to their probable falsity. If you find that statements in the letter are consistent with and are corroborated by other, substantial pre-publication evidence of Halevy's state of mind, then you may consider these statements and give them such weight, if any, as they may deserve in deciding whether Halevy acted prior to publication with actual malice. On the other hand, if you find that statements in the letter are inconsistent with or are uncorroborated by substantial pre-publication evidence of Halevy's state of mind, then you may not consider those statements in deciding whether Halevy acted with actual malice. If you consider this letter, you should also consider the fact that the letter was written 17 months after Mr. Halevy wrote his World Wide Memo item and 15 months after publication of the challenged paragarph, and that Minister Sharon had filed his lawsuits over the Article prior to Mr. Halevy's writing this letter. You can also consider Mr. Halevy's statements about Minister Sharon prior to publication of the Article at issue, including his statement that Sharon is a "remarkable military leader, an outstanding statesman" (Tr. 960), as well as his other statements that Sharon was a "ruthless leader" with a "naked ambition for power" (Tr. 953), and all other relevant evidence.

In considering the paragraph at issue, keep in mind that plaintiff cannot prevail merely because you may believe that Time presented a one-sided or unbalanced account of the facts in question. Similarly, actual malice cannot be established by acts of negligence or mistake. If Time's employees were negligent in the way they reported, wrote, edited, or checked the Article, and if those employees failed to act as reasonably prudent reporters, writers, or editor should — in other words, if they were merely careless — this evidence may be considered by you in deciding the actual malice question. But lack of balance, negligence, or carelessness, would not in themselves be sufficient to allow plaintiff to recover. Although negligence may be alone sufficient to sustain a claim in other circumstances, in this special case, where freedom of speech is involved, plaintiff must satisfy the higher burden of showing actual malice, as I have defined it.

On the question of actual malice, you may consider publications which Time personnel claim they read and relied on in publishing the paragraph at issue. In order for you to give any weight to a particular article on the question of actual malice, you must first find that someone at Time actually read the article before Time's February 21 story was published. Second, you must consider whether someone who read a particular article in fact relied upon what he or she read. If you find that the witness did not rely upon the relevant portion of the article, then you should not consider reliance on the article as evidence of lack of actual malice. If, however, you find that the witness honestly relied upon what he or she read, then you may consider that reliance as evidence on the issue of actual malice. When you are assessing the credibility of a witness' testimony that he or she read and relied on a statement in a particular article, you should consider all the relevant evidence, including the witness' consistency, demeanor, and bias; evidence concerning the reliability of the story; and the story itself, including its tone and content. It is important, however, that you consider these factors only in deciding whether a witness actually and subjectively believed and relied upon the article. In other words, it is not enough that *you* would not have believed that an article was true, or that *you* would have had serious doubts about the truth of Time's story after reading other publications. The actual malice issue turns on whether the people at Time who prepared the story and paragraph at issue had such doubts.

In determining whether any Time employee acted with actual malice, you should consider the evidence concerning Minister Sharon's public testimony before the Commission. You must decide on the issue of actual malice whether any responsible Time employee honestly believed, prior to the publication of the paragraph at issue, that Sharon had publicly admitted on October 25, 1982 before the Kahan Commission that had discussed revenge with the Gemayels, presumably at Bikfaya. If you find, for example, that Halevy honestly believed that Sharon testified publicly that he had discussed revenge with the Gemayels, then that belief could alone satisfy you that plaintiff has failed to prove Halevy acted with actual malice in representing in the World Wide Memo of December 6, 1982 the fact that Sharon discussed revenge with the Gemayels. Similarly, Harry Kelly has testified that he relied on two English translations of Sharon's public testimony, and that he understood Sharon to be referring in these two translations to discussion about revenge at Bikfaya. If you believe this testimony, you may give it such weight as you think it deserves with respect to Kelly's state of mind, and in deciding whether plaintiff has shown by clear and convincing evidence that Kelly in fact entertained serious doubts about the truth of Time Magazine's story. On the other hand, if you disbelieved the testimony of either Halevy or Kelly as to the meaning to them of Sharon's public testimony before the Kahan Commission, then you may consider your disbelief in deciding whether they acted with actual malice, or on any other issue to which their credibility is relevant. Remember that, even if you find that Kelly or any other responsible Time employee honestly believed that Sharon testified publicly to a discussion of revenge with the Gemayels at Bikfaya, you may still have to decide whether any responsible Time employee acted with actual malice in stating that Time had learned that details of the alleged discussion were in Appendix B. The latter finding will be necessary in the event that you conclude that the statement about Appendix B aggravated the defamatory effect of the paragraph at issue.

In deciding what Time's responsible employees actually believed about Minister Sharon's public testimony before the Commission, you will obviously have to consider the credibility of Mr. Halevy, of Mr. Kelly, of Minister Sharon, and of the other witnesses whose testimony you may find pertinent. Furthermore, you should consider the documentary evi-

Appendix 4 — Sharon Jury Instructions

dence presented to you that pertains to this question, including the context of Minister Sharon's testimony, the Commission Report, the manner in which Time Magzine interpreted Sharon's public testimony in its article of November 8, 1982, the manner in which Halevy or Kelly treated the issue of a discussion between Sharon and the Gemayels in the World Wide Memo of December 6, 1982 and in "Take 9" of the story at issue in this case, any relevant testimony of Time employees other than Halevy and Kelly, and the extent to which Time treated as significant in the paragraph at issue and in its press release the fact that Time had learned of a discussion of revenge between Sharon and the Gemayels. You should also consider any evidence you have heard about the meaning of the Hebrew word "etzlenu," keeping mind that Halevy, but no other Time employee, read the Hebrew version of the testimony before he read any English report.

In deciding the issue of actual malice you should consider the testimony of Time personnel as to what they in fact believed about Sharon's culpability for the massacre when Time's article was published. Time contends that none of its employees has testified that he or she believed at the time of publication that Sharon, when he ordered the Phalangists to enter Sabra and Shatilla, consciously intended to allow or encouraged acts of revenge extending to the deliberate killing of noncombatants. You may find that the paragraph was defamatory in a way that one or more employees at Time has admitted he or she in fact did not believe. Standing alone, this apparent incongruity does not constitute actual malice. The Time employees who admitted that they did not believe that Minister Sharon consciously intended to allow or encouraged acts of revenge extending to the deliberate killing of noncombatants, also testified that they did not believe that the paragraph stated, either of those two actionable defamatory meanings, by implication or otherwise. If you find that a Time employee honestly believed at the time of publication that the paragraph did not state by implication a defamatory meaning which conflicted with his or her beliefs concerning Sharon's culpability, then you must find that the employee did not act with actual malice, even if you determine that the employee interpreted the paragraph incorrectly. Actual malice requires proof of knowing falsity, or of a high degree of awareness of probable falsity. A person who genuinely believes he or she is not making a particular defamatory statement cannot be found to have consciously falsified, or to have been aware of probable falsity, in making that statement. On the other hand, if plaintiff proves by clear and convincing evidence that a Time employee responsible for a statement about plaintiff in fact was aware that the average reader would have construed the statement as defamatory in the relevant sense, then you should find that the employee acted with actual malice if he or she did not believe that Sharon was culpable in the degree conveyed by the defamatory statement.

You have heard the parties argue why you should or should not find actual malice in this case. I will not restate all those arguments. I will tell you, however, without intending to cover all the possibilities, what types of findings could lead you to render a verdict that Time acted with actual malice. Once again, you should draw no inferences whatever from this effort to provide you guidance in rendering your verdict. You and you alone must decide what answers to give to the issues posed.

First, and most obviously, you should find actual malice if you determine that Halevy or Kelly fabricated any of the factual claims in the paragraph at issue what provides the basis for any actionable defamatory statement you may find was made about plaintiff. Even if you find that Halevy or other employees at Time genuinely believed that Minister Sharon must somehow have known in advance that the Phalangists would massacre Palestinians in Sabra and Shatilla, you may nevertheless find that Time acted with actual malice if Halevy or any such employee simply made up the allegation that Sharon discussed with the Gemayels at Bikfaya the need to take revenge for the death of Bashir. You may also find actual malice if an employee simply made up the claim that Appendix B contains details of that alleged discussion, in the event you have determined that this factual claim materially aggravated the paragraph's defamatory effect. The relevant inquiry for you is whether Halevy, Kelly, or any other responsible Time employee knew that any of the facts that constituted the basis for implying defamatory statements about plaintiff was false, or whether any of them had serious doubts as to the truth of such facts, however genuinely he may have believed in the truth of the underlying message you find the alleged facts conveyed. Thus, you may find actual malice if you find that Halevy lied about the existence of the sources who he said gave him the facts that he and Kelly conveyed to Time, or that Halevy lied about his sources told him, or as to having been read or having seen the minutes of the Bikfaya meeting, if you conclude that these findings demonstrate that Halevy therefore either knew that the paragraph ultimately published in Time was materially false, or that he recklessly disregarded its probable falsity. You may, in short, reject a profession of good faith, by Halevy or anyone else at Time, if you find that facts were fabricated. On the other hand, if you find that Halevy testified truthfully as to his sources, and that Kelly and the others at Time believed what Halevy told them, you should find no actual malice on this ground, even if you find Halevy or others were negligent or were honestly misled.

Second, you may find actual malice if the plaintiff has proved that Halevy, Kelly, Smith, or others at Time so greatly exaggerated or distorted the information they actually received about Minister Sharon that at least one of them must have known that a defamatory fact published in the paragraph at issue was false or probably false. In determining this question, keep in mind that a reporter or writer is constitutionally protected against liability for adding any analysis or interpretation, unless he acts with actual malice. You should compare the information you believe that Halevy actually received with the information ultimately published in Time. If you fnd a material difference between what Halevy actually learned and what ultimately was published, which produced a defamatory effect of greater impact, and if you also find that Halevy or another Time employee knew that the difference was probably a false statement, then you should render a verdict for plaintiff on this theory. If you find no material difference, or a difference that produced a lesser defamatory effect, or if you find a material difference but conclude that plaintiff has failed to prove that a responsible Time employee knew that the difference as published represented a statement that was false or probably false, then you should render a verdict for defendant on this theory.

Third, plaintiff has suggested that Time acted with actual malice because Time personnel responsible for the paragraph at issue consciously disregarded substantial evidence that the paragraph at issue was incorrect in material respects. Plaintiff claims that the paragraph at issue was written in a defamatory manner because Kelly and others at Time wanted to write a "scoop" about what was in Appendix B; and that responsible persons at Time at all points prior to publication deliberately disregarded the possibility that Halevy could have misled them as to the truth. Time's posture, plaintiff has argued, led responsible persons at Time to disregard, prior to publication, evidence that indicated that material facts in the paragraph at issue were false or probably false, including: alleged differences between what Halevy said he learned and what was ultimately published; alleged evidence that Halevy was biased against Minister Sharon and the Likud leadership, and that this bias may have led him to publish false facts in the past; and evidence in the Commission Report as published which plaintiff claims indicated that Halevy's alleged information and the published story might be wrong, including the Commission's statements on the extent of plaintiff's responsibility for the massacre, and the fact that the public portion of the Commission's Report appeared to have attributed no significance to the meeting at Bikfaya.

If you find that plaintiff has proved by clear and convincing evidence that Time's personnel systematically disregarded substantial evidence that any material fact as published in the paragraph at issue was untrue, you may also be led to find that one or more of Time's personnel responsible for the story in fact disbelieved or seriously doubted the relevant facts but simply disregarded them. On the other hand, you have heard testimony that Time personnel check stories carefully, that they relied on Halevy and found his stories accurate, and the reasons why they found the believability of the paragraph at issue was not adversely affected by statements in the public portion of the Commission report. If you find that plaintiff has failed to prove that any responsible person at Time disregarded substantial evidence of falsity, or that plaintiff has failed to prove, for whatever reason, that a responsible person at Time in fact seriously doubted the truth of the relevant facts in the paragraph, then you may not find for plaintiff. Keep in mind that, while you may consider what responsible persons at

Time did, and the objective circumstances of which you find they must have known, you can find actual malice only if plaintiff has proved by clear and convincing evidence that a responsible person at Time in fact knew the paragraph was false in some material respect or had a high degree of awareness of its probable falsity.

In determining whether Time acted with actual malice on this third theory, you should consider Time's contention that it relied upon facts gathered by a professional journalist who Time claims it believed had a proven track record for accuracy and reliability. If you find, for example, that Time personnel did regard Halevy as an accurate and reliable journalist, and as a result no responsible Time employee had substantial doubts about the accuracy of the facts Halevy reported, then you must return a verdict for defendant on this third theory of actual malice. On the other hand, if you find that plaintiff has shown that, despite Halevy's contributions to Time, his track record in fact led one or more responsible Time employees to have substantial doubts about the accuracy of the paragraph at issue, then you must return a verdict for plaintiff on this theory of actual malice.

This brings me to the end of my instructions on the issues that you should consider at this stage in the proceedings. We have deferred any consideration by you of the issues relating to plaintiff's claim that he was damaged, and you should put aside that question at this point. We have done this for reasons that should not concern you, and you should draw no inference one way or the other from this division of the issues. In the meantime, you must disregard entirely any evidence you have heard that relates solely to the plaintiff's reputation or alleged damages. The lawyers will remind you of that evidence in the event you reach the questions of damages and reputation, and I will give you an additional charge on those subjects.

IV. EVALUATION OF EVIDENCE

During this trial I have occasionally instructed you to consider or not to consider evidence for one purpose or another. If you perceive any inconsistency between anything I said to you about the admissibility of any testimony or exhibit during the trial, and what I have told you in these instructions, you should disregard what I said to you before and give controlling weight to these instructions. You must be sure to use evidence only for authorized purposes. You would violate your oath as jurors to do otherwise.

The fact that I permit you to consider testimony, an article, or other evidence on one or more issues does not mean that you must give it any weight in deciding the issue or issues involved. It is up to you, as finders of the facts, to decide what weight to give any evidence that I allow you to consider. Thus, for example, you are free to conclude that a particular article is entitled to weight on actual malice, or on the other hand to conclude that no one could reasonably have relied on it in any pertinent respect. In short, although you may consider any evidence I tell you is admissible, *you* must decide what, if any, weight the evidence should be given.

I can give you no magical formula by which you should evaluate testimony or other evidence. You bring with you to this courtroom all of the experience and background of your lives, including your commonsense. In your everyday affairs you regularly determine for yourselves the reliability or unreliability of statements made by others. The same tests that you use in your everyday dealings are the tests you should apply in your deliberations.

You have, in general, heard two types of evidence in this case: direct evidence, such as eyewitness testimony; and circumstantial evidence — that is, proof of a set of circumstances that point to certain facts. The law does not distinguish between these two types of evidence; in principle, one type of evidence is as good as the other. The law simply requires that you find the facts in accordance with all the evidence in the case, both direct and circumstantial.

The evidence in the case consists of the sworn testimony of the witnesses, all exhibits received in evidence, and all facts that have been admitted or stipulated. Comments and arguments of counsel, whether made in their opening or closing statements or during the course of the trial, are not evidence in the case. Anything you may have seen or heard outside the courtroom is not evidence and must be disregarded.

As the sole judges of the facts, you must determine which of the witnesses you believe, what portion of their testimony you accept, and what weight you attach to any testimony. At times during the trial I sustained objections to questions without permitting the witness to answer, or I instructed that an answer be stricken from the record or that you disregard it. You may draw no inference from an unanswered question, nor may you consider testimony that has been stricken. The law requires that your decision be made solely upon the competent evidence before you. On the other hand, you are not limited to what you see and hear as the witnesses testify. You are permitted to draw, from facts that you find have been proved, such reasonable inferences as you feel are justified in the light of your experience.

Use your commonsense in evaluating the evidence. You have watched the witnesses testify. How did each witness impress you? Did he or she seem to be telling the truth? Was the substance of his or her testimony credible? Consider the witness' demeanor on the stand — that his, his or her conduct and manner. Consider the witness' ability to perceive, recall, and narrate accurately. Take into account any contradictory statements that the witness made, either before you or in earlier testimony. If a witness willfully testified falsely as to any material fact, either at this trial or at a deposition, then you may disregard his or her testimony entirely, or you may accept any portion of the testimony that you believe and reject such portions as you disbelieve. In weighing the effect of a discrepancy, always consider whether it pertains to a matter of importance or to an unimportant detail, and whether the discrepancy results from innocent error or failure of recollection, or from intentional falsehood. You are the sole judges of what weight, if any, to give to particular testimony or documents.

Evidence that at some other time a witness who is not a party to this action may have said something inconsistent with the witness' testimony at the trial, may in general be considered only in judging the credibility of the witness, and not as evidence or proof of the truth of any such statement. If the witness is a party to the case, however, which includes Minister Sharon and all employees of Time, and if by the statement the witness admits some facts or facts against his interest, then the statement, if knowingly made, may be considered as evidence of the truth of the fact or facts admitted, and also may be considered for the purpose of judging credibility. Furthermore, the deposition testimony of a party can be introduced to prove the truth or falsity of any statement the testimony contains.

Many of the witnesses in this case have an interest in its outcome, including the plaintiff and the employees of Time. A witness' interest in the outcome of the case does not by itself mean that he or she has not told the truth. It is for you to determine, from observing the testimony, as well as from considering any testimony or other evidence which may seem to contradict that testimony, and your own experience, whether or not the witness' interest has affected his or her testimony. You are not required to disbelieve an interested witness, and you may accept any part of such testimony which you deem reliable and reject all or any party which you deem unworthy of acceptance.

During the trial you also heard several hypothetical questions, based on assumed facts. This is a proper technique, designed to enable you to evaluate the position and/or credibility of a witness. You should keep in mind, however, that the accuracy and relevance of the assumed facts may have a bearing on the weight you might care to give any answers to such questions.

Some testimony in this trial came from an expert witness, Ms. Kuslansky. A witness who, by education and experience, has become expert in some profession or calling may state her opinions as to matters within the area of her expertise, and may also state reasons for the opinions. You should give any expert opinion received in evidence such weight as you think it deserves. If you decide that an expert witness' opinion is not based upon sufficient education and experience, or if you conclude that the reasons given in support of the opinion are not sound, or if you feel that the expert opinion is irrelevant or outweighed by other evidence, then you may disregard the opinion entirely, or give it such weight as you feel it deserves. If you find, however, that the expert was qualified and testified persuasively, you may credit the testimony in your deliberations.

In the questioning of certain witnesses, testimony has been read to you from depositions, consisting of sworn answers to questions asked of the witness in advance of the trial. Such testimony is entitled to the same consideration as live testimony, and you should evalute any contradictions between a witness' live testimony and deposition testimony just as you would evaluate discrepancies in the live testimony. As I told you during the trial, every witness at a deposition is sworn to tell the entire truth, and you may consider any changes or additions in the testimony of a witness at trial in evaluating the witness' credibility. You may, however, take into account the possibility that differences between live testimony and deposition testimony resulted from the passage of time, or from differences in the questions that were asked at deposition and at trial.

During the trial, witnesses for both parties have raised claims of privilege as a basis for not responding to particular questions. The law recognizes certain privileges in order to protect various interests and relationships that are regarded as sufficiently important to justify the sacrifice of relevant information. Thus, for example, Minister Sharon, David Halevy, and others have refused to answer certain questions on the ground that to do so would violate Israeli secrecy laws. Israeli law prohibits the disclosure of various forms of confidential, nonpublication information, and makes such disclosure a violation of Israeli laws. Minister Sharon, or David Halevy, or any other witness in this trial who possesses such confidential information is privileged not to answer any question that would require him to reveal that information in violation of Israeli law. In addition, Mr. Halevy and Mr. Kelly have refused to answer certain questions on the ground that to do so would require them, as reporters, to reveal confidential sources. New York law confers upon the press a right to keep their sources confidential, and Mr. Halevy and other Time employees are privileged to refuse to disclose the names of Halevy's sources or other identifying information about them.

The question whether a privilege is fairly invoked — that is, whether the witness refusing to respond has a legally recognized privilege not to answer the question posed — is a question of law and, as such, is for me to decide. Whenever each of these privileges was properly invoked during the trial, the witness was not required to respond.

You are not permitted to give any evidentiary weight to a witness' refusal to respond to a question on the basis of a privilege I have found to apply. For example, if a witness who is a reporter properly refused to answer a question on the ground that his answer would reveal identifying information about one of his sources, you may not rely on the fact of his refusal as a basis for inferring anything about whether or not he had a source, or what the source said, or the source's reliability. The proper assertion of this privilege may not be penalized. Similarly, when Minister Sharon invoked Israeli secrecy law as a basis for refusing to answer questions about the contents of the secret Appendix, or of other confidential information or documents, you may not infer anything from the mere fact of his refusal.

On the other hand, you must, of course, decide the issues in this case. While the invocation of neither privilege with which we are dealing here may be penalized, you must keep in mind that plaintiff has the burden of proof on all three issues before you, and his reliance on the privilege cannot to any extent whatever lighten his evidentiary obligations. Furthermore, and with respect to both Sharon and Halevy, while a party's failure to present evidence may be privileged, the record will nevertheless lack the evidence withheld, and must be judged without the benefit of such evidence. Thus, although I have ruled that Minister Sharon justifiably refused to testify to the contents of certain secret documents, you still must find the relevant facts about the contents of such documents, and will have to do so without the evidence he might otherwise have provided. You may find the lack of evidence on a particular issue significant or insignificant, depending on the question involved, the relationship of the question and information sought to the issues in the case, the other evidence available to you to decide the issue, and the burden of proof that applies. Similarly, although Mr. Halevy justifiably refused to testify about the identity of his alleged sources, and although you may not hold against him the fact of his invocation of the reporter's privilege, you must nevertheless decide whether you believe that he had a given source, whether he obtained what he believed to be reliable information from his sources, and whether he believed the information he received in fact supported the statements made by Time. The privilege only prevents you from using the mere fact of the witness' refusal to reveal information as evidence, and it does not require you to accept the witness' credibility.

Each of you is entitled to his or her own opinion. Until now, I have told you not to discuss this case with anyone.

Now, you are required to exchange views with your fellow jurors. That is the purpose of jury deliberations. Remember that you are not partisans, but judges of the facts. It is your duty, as jurors, to consult with one another and to deliberate with a view to reaching an agreeement, if you can do so without violence to your individual judgment. If you have a particular point of view, but discussions with your fellow jurors make you think that your view may be wrong, do not hesitate to change your mind. The jury cannot function if any of you refuses to listen to other jurors with an open mind. But you should not change a position that you conscientiously believe just because you are outnumbered. You should accept an opposing position only if you are convinced that it satisfies your judgment and conscience.

You will begin your deliberations in a few moments. To return a verdict, you must be unanimous — all six of you must agree. Jury unanimity is an important feature of our system of justice, for it increases confidence in jury verdicts. I will send with you a form on which to record your verdict, as well as answers to certain questions. That form is drafted to enable you to record any verdict that you could possibly reach, so you should not treat the inclusion of particular questions on the form as suggesting what your decision should be. You must answer each question on the form carefully, so we can know the bases for your decisions. In rendering your verdict, you may of course consider and discuss all the issues on which you have been instructed, but I am asking you to render a verdict on one issue at a time. Thus, when you reach a verdict on the issue of defamatory meaning you should send your verdict and findings to me in a sealed envelope. I will then instruct you as to your next assignment.

In the course of your discussions you should remember that your recollection controls as to what was said and done in the courtroom. You are not bound by anything said to you about the record by the lawyers or by me. If during your deliberations you are in doubt as to what was said during the trial by any witness, you may ask to have the relevant portion or portions of the transcript read to you in court. Please feel free to ask to have portions of the testimony read to you, but do so only if you in fact need to hear the testimony. Furthermore, be as specific as possible in your requests to hear testimony, since the process takes time.

If, in the course of your deliberations, you should find yourself in doubt concerning my instructions to you on the law, you may refer to the written charge, six copies of which I am sending into the jury room with you. When and if you decide to refer to the written instructions, keep in mind that you must consider the instructions I have given you as a whole. Don't take anything I have said out of context. Furthermore, if you need any clarification of any rule of law, or you need an answer to any question as to the law that arises in your deliberations, then send me a note explaining the problem, and I will do my best to answer.

You have the right to see any exhibit properly admissible on the issue you have under consideration. I am not sending any exhibit into the jury room with you as you begin your deliberations. I am sending in with you, however, a list of all exhibits in evidence, and you may ask for the exhibits you wish to see simply by sending a note to me through your foreperson, via the Marshal. Any question you may have should likewise be sent to me in a note, via the Marshal, and I will do my best to answer it.

APPENDIX 5

Sharon v. Time

Jury Verdict Form

We the jury unanimously render the following verdict with respect to the issues in this case:

I. DEFAMATORY MEANING

Has plaintiff proved by a preponderance of the evidence that a statement or statements in the challenged paragraph in the Article "The Verdict is Guilty," read in context, defame plaintiff in some actionable manner as definded by the instructions on this subject?

Yes _____
No _____

FINDINGS ON DEFAMATORY MEANING

If you find that plaintiff has proved that the paragraph at issue contains an actionable defamatory statement or statements, as defined by the instructions, then indicate which of the following defamatory meaning or meanings the paragraph contains. (You may find more than one defamatory meaning.)

1. The paragraph in context states that, in permitting the Phalangists to enter Sabra and Shatilla, Minister Sharon consciously intended to permit the Phalangists to take acts of revenge extending to the deliberate killing of noncombatants in the camps.

_____ Yes

_____ No

2. The paragraph in context states that, in permitting the Phalangists to enter Sabra and Shatilla, Minister Sharon actively encouraged the Phalangists in their intention to commit acts of revenge in Sabra and Shatilla extending to the deliberate killing of noncombatants.

_____ Yes

_____ No

If you find that Time's paragraph contained either of the defamatory meanings set out above, was the defamatory effect of the paragraph aggravated by Time's statement that details of the alleged conversation were contained in Appendix B of the Commission Report?

_____ Yes

_____ No

II. FALSITY

Has plaintiff proved by clear and convincing evidence the falsity of the facts in the paragraph that imply the defamatory statement or statements you found Time made?

_____ Yes

_____ No

FINDINGS WITH RESPECT TO FALSITY

In rendering your verdict on falsity, keep in mind that defendant has conceded that plaintiff has proved by clear and convincing evidence that Appendix B of the Commission Report contains no details of a discussion by Minister Sharon with the Phalangists, prior to the massacre, of the need to take revenge for the death of Bashir Gemayel. You need therefore answer only the following question:

1. Has plaintiff proved by clear and convincing evidence that he did not engage in any discussion with Phalangists, prior to the massacre, of the need to take revenge for the death of Bashir Gemayel?
_____ Yes
_____ No

III. ACTUAL MALICE

Has plaintiff proved by clear and convincing evidence that a person or persons at Time, Inc. responsible for either reporting, writing, editing, or publishing the paragraph at issue did so with actual malice, in that he, she, or they knew, at the time of publishing any statement you have found was false and defamatory, that the defamatory statement was false or had serious doubts as to its truth?
_____ Yes
_____ No

FINDINGS ON ACTUAL MALICE

If you find that plaintiff has proved actual malice, please indicate the basis or bases upon which you have reached that verdict.

1. Plaintiff has proved by clear and convincing evidence that Halevy or some other responsible Time employee knowingly fabricated the evidence in any manner so that he or any other responsible employee was aware that the paragraph was false or that it was probably untrue.
_____ Yes
_____ No

If your answer is "Yes," please specify which fact or facts were known to be false or probably untrue:
_____ The statement that plaintiff engaged in a discussion with the Gemayels at Bikfaya of the need to take revenge.
_____ The statement that details of that discussion are contained in Appendix B.
_____ Both of the above.

2. Plaintiff has proved by clear and convincing evidence that Halevy, or Kelly, or Smith, or any other responsible Time employee, materially exaggerated or distorted the information Halevy actually received, so that at least one responsible Time employee was in fact aware that the paragraph as published was false or probably untrue.
_____ Yes
_____ No

If your answer to this question is "Yes," please specify which fact or facts were known to be false or probably untrue:
_____ The statement that plaintiff engaged in a discussion with the Gemayels at Bikfaya of the need to take revenge.
_____ The statement that details of that discussion are contained in Appendix B.
_____ Both of the above.

3. Plaintiff has proved by clear and convincing evidence that, because of Time's policies and practices, Time's personnel disregarded substantial evidence of the probable falsity of the paragraph at issue, although the evidence must in fact have caused at least one responsible Time employee to become aware that the paragraph as published was false or probably untrue.
_____ Yes
_____ No

If your answer to this question is "Yes," please specify which fact or facts were known to be false or probably untrue:
_____ The statement that plaintiff engaged in a discussion with the Gemayels at Bikfaya of the need to take revenge.
_____ The statement that details of that discussion are contained in Appendix B.
_____ Both of the above.

4. If you find that actual malice has been proved on some basis other than described above, please say so below and describe the basis for your finding.

APPENDIX 6

Sharon v. Time

Juror Questionnaire

No. _____

JURORS MUST BE SWORN BEFORE COMPLETING THIS QUESTIONNAIRE

The furnishing of information on this questionnaire is designed to expedite the jury selection process in this case. In most cases the questions can be answered by placing an "X" in the proper box. If you have any inquiries concerning any particular question, please contact the court and it will be explained to you.

1. Name
2. The case for which this questionnaire is being completed is one in which the plaintiff, Ariel Sharon, former Defense Minister of the State of Israel, is suing the defendant, Time Magazine, Inc., for libel. The suit will involve consideration of the events leading up to the massacre of Palestinian civilians by Christian Phalangists in the refugee camps at Sabra and Shatilla, located in West Beirut, Lebanon.

The parties in this case are entitled to a fair trial, which means in part that every juror selected in this case be fair and impartial. To be qualified, a juror must be able to rest his or her verdict on the evidence, must abide by all instructions and rulings of the judge, and must have no bias, prejudice, or belief that interferes with the juror's fairness and impartiality.

Keeping in mind the nature in this case, the parties involved, and the factual context, can you serve fairly and impartially, resting your verdict strictly on the evidence and the law?
( ) Yes
( ) No
If your answer is "No," you may stop completing this form and return it to the Jury Clerk. If your answer is "Yes," please go on to the next question.

3. Age
Where were you born?
4. Where did you grow up?
5. Town and County of present Residence
6. How long have you lived at your residence?
7. Do you:
( ) Own
( ) Rent
( ) Live with relatives or friends
8. Are you or any of your close friends or relatives of Arab, Palestinian, Lebanese, Muslim, Israeli, or Jewish heritage?
( ) Yes
( ) No
If yes, explain
9. What is the highest grade of schooling you have finished?
( ) 8th grade or less
( ) some high school
( ) high school graduate
( ) community college
( ) some four year college
( ) college graduate
( ) post graduate
If you have education/training beyond high school, please list the field(s) of study:
10. What civic, educational, professional, sports, business, religious or political activities do you participate in?

11. Have you held any office in any organization, and if so, what office?
12. Do you read a newspaper regularly (at least two or three times a week)?
   ( ) Yes
   ( ) No
   If yes, list the names of the newspapers you read and indicate how often you read each newspaper.
13. What magazines or periodicals do you read?
14. What TV programs, if any, do you watch regularly?
15. If you have any hobbies, please list them below.
16. Are you:
   ( ) Employed full-time
   ( ) Employed part-time
   ( ) Homemaker
   ( ) Unemployed or laid off
   ( ) Retired
   ( ) Student
   ( ) Disabled
   (a) If employed full-time or part-time, what *type* of work do you do for a living?
   (b) If retired or unemployed, what type of work had you been doing?
   (c) If homemaker or student, have you a job skill which you have worked at?
      ( ) Yes
      ( ) No
      If yes, what?
17. If employed, unemployed, or retired, list the name of our current (last) employer:
   (a) What is (was) your job title?
   (b) What are (were) your duties on that job?
   (c) Do (did) you supervise others in that job?
      ( ) Yes
      ( ) No
      If yes, how many?
18. Do you have a second job?
   ( ) Yes
   ( ) No
   If so, what do you do?
19. Are you:
   ( ) Single, never married
   ( ) Married
   ( ) Divorced/separated
   ( ) Widow/widower
20. How many children do you have, if any?
   List the sex, age and occupation of each employed child:
21. If you have *ever* been married, list your spouse's most recent *type of work* and *place of employment:*

22. Have you, a member of your family, or a good friend ever served in the military?
   ( ) Yes
   ( ) No
   If yes, list the following information:
      Relation to you
      Branch
      Years
      Place
      Job/Rank
23. Have you ever been called for jury duty before?
   ( ) Yes
   ( ) No
   If yes, please use the following chart to describe the type of jury service (work from the most recent case back).
      CASE NO.
      COURT (state/federal)
      JURY (trial/grand)
      CASE (criminal/civil)
      REACH A VERDICT (Yes/No)
24. Have you ever appeared as a witness in court, or given a statement under oath in any type of legal proceeding?
   ( ) Yes
   ( ) No
   If yes, please describe the circumstances:
25. Have you, or a member of your family ever brought a lawsuit against another individual, or against a corporation?
   ( ) Yes
   ( ) No
   If yes, please describe the circumstance, and the outcome for each lawsuit:
26. Have you, or a member of your family ever had a lawsuit brought against you?
   ( ) Yes
   ( ) No
   If yes, please describe the circumstances and outcome of each lawsuit:
27. Have you, or anyone you know *well*, ever RECEIVED TRAINING, or been EMPLOYED in any of the following areas? (Circle as many as apply for each category.)
   a. Law/Law enforcement/Court system [self, close relative, close friend]
   b. News Industry or Publication [self, close relative, close friend]
   c. Military [self, close relative, close friend]
   d. Religious Organization or Activity [self, close relative, close friend]
28. Do you have any problem with your hearing or vision that would prevent you

Appendix 6 — Sharon Juror Questionnaire

from giving full attention to all of the evidence at this trial?
( ) Yes
( ) No
29. Do you have any difficulty in reading or understanding English?
( ) Yes
( ) No
30. Do you read, speak or understand any language other than English?
( ) Yes
( ) No
If yes, which one[s]
31. Have you ever written a "letter to the editor" to any newspaper or magazine?
( ) Yes
( ) No
Explain the circumstances
32. Have you ever made a contribution to or financially supported the State of Israel or any Arab State?
( ) Yes
( ) No
33. Have you ever visited the Middle East?
( ) Yes
( ) No
If yes, when, where and for how long?
34. Do you have any opinion or bias concerning lawyers that could interfere with your service as a juror in this case?
( ) Yes
( ) No
35. The parties in the cae in which you are being called are represented by the firms of Shea & Gould and Cravath, Swaine & Moore. Do you know anyone currently or previously employed by or affiliated with those firms?
( ) Yes
( ) No
36. Do you know any of the following lawyers?
  Milton Gould
  Bernard Fishman
  Arnold Forster
  Richard Goldstein
  Adam Gilbert
  Andrea Feller
  Thomas Barr
  Robert Rifkind
  Paul Saunders
  Stuart Gold
  Kathleen Beggs
  Israel Leshem
  Stephen Madsen
  Ellen Oran
  Anne Verdon
  William Guttman
  Harry Johnston
  Robert Marshall

37. Do you know (*i.e.*, have you met) any of the following persons?
  Ariel Sharon
  Uri Dan
  Brian Brown
  Ray Cave
  Helen Doyle
  Richard Duncan
  Nellie Gonzalez
  Henry Grunwald
  David Halevy
  Harry Kelly
  John Meyers
  Henry Muller
  Robert Slater
  William Smith
  Robert Parker
  Ray Cline
  Alfonse D'Amato
  George Keegan
  Robert Morgenthau
  Bayard Rustin
  Leon Uris
  William Van Cleave
  Elmo Zumwalt
  Josette Alia
  Abraham Allsberg
  Swee Chai Ang
  Shayke Baitel
  Chaim Bar-Lev
  Wiebke Bruhns
  Patti Chamoun
  Helena Cobban
  Amnon Cohen
  Morris Draper
  Amir Drori
  Moshe Elul
  Gunnar Flagstar
  Sonia Frangieh
  Rudi Frey
  Avshalom Graboswky
  John Harbo
  Moshe Hevroni
  Dan Horowitz
  David Kimche
  Klaus Liedtke
  Marjaleena Oray
  Richard Parker
  William Quandt
  Yehoshua Saguy
  Harold Saunders
  Ellen Siegel
  William Stewart
  Mary Suro
  Robert Suro
  Dov Tamari
  Ron Ben-Yishai
38. Do you regularly take any medication?
( ) Yes
( ) No

If yes, describe
39. Have you or any member of your family been charged with a crime?
( ) Yes
( ) No
40. This case will take about four weeks to try. We will not be sitting on religious holidays, and every reasonable effort will be made to accommodate the special needs of individual jurors. We will also not sit on Friday afternoons. Of course, you realize that mere inconvenience or the usual financial hardships connected with jury service will not be a sufficient reason to excuse a prospective juror. In light of these considerations, would service in this case create any *serious hardship* for you?
( ) Yes
( ) No
If yes, explain:

———————————